THE LAUGHING AUDIENCE

Paul Iles

THE SCOTTISH MUSIC HALL
1880 - 1990

THE
SCOTTISH
MUSIC HALL

1880 - 1990

by

J. H. LITTLEJOHN

ACKNOWLEDGEMENTS

People's Palace Museum, Glasgow — Metropol Interior.
Clydebank District Council — Clydebank Pavilion Playbill.

I wish to record my indebtedness to the many individuals and public bodies whose unstinted co-operation facilitated the research and publication of this book. Also acknowledged is the zeal for the project expressed by those in Variety who provided photographs and playbills.

J. H. LITTLEJOHN,
Edinburgh.
July, 1990.

G. C. Book Publishers Ltd.
10 Bank Street, Wigtown, Wigtownshire, DG8 9HP
Telephones: 098 84 3215/2499

Published 1990

Printed by The Northern Times Ltd.,
Main Street, Golspie, Sutherland, Scotland.

ISBN 1 872350 05 4

Contents

Plates

Foreword

For lovers of the Scottish Music Hall this book is a treasure trove of fond memories. This is history with a heart the heart of variety.

Jimmy Littlejohn's thorough documentation of the "Halls", as they were affectionately known, takes us from the Golden Age of the Music Hall right through to its declining years. But in Scotland at least still gallantly clinging on. Older readers, especially, will delight in remembrance of regular weekly visits to these Palaces of Laughter.

I am especially pleased that honourable mention has been generously given to so many artistes, who were perhaps lesser well known than their Top of the Bill contemporaries. It is right and fitting, that their contributions should be recorded and indeed applauded.

Robert Wilson was the man who gave me my start in the business in 1952. How lucky can you get? What an artiste and what a gentleman. Then in 1960 Eric Popplewell invited me to succeed the great Jack Milroy as comic in the Ayr Gaiety Whirl. It was then I realised the benefit of my previous association with fine comedians like Stan Mars, Tommy Loman, Aly Wilson, George Burton and Pete Martin, and the pleasure of appearing with talented ladies like Alice Dale and Anne Fields. Joyful memories also of working with two great comedy characters — John Mulvaney and Hector Nicol. Happily the Gaiety Theatre in Ayr under the efficient stewardship of Bernard Cotton still proudly flies the flag of Variety.

The book is a worthy tribute to the many performers whose names fill its pages. Their philosophy was, "you don't just watch a live show, you're in it!" Theirs was a labour of love. The author has done them proudly. On behalf of all the "Pros", past and present who feature in these chapters, well done Jimmy!

As we say in the business — "Happy for Tabs"!

Johnny Beattie

Johnny Beattie.

This book is dedicated to Margaret.

Chapter
One

"*European Cultural Capital*"

Glasgow

Glasgow

Precursors of the Music Hall in Glasgow were licensed singing saloons and concert taverns comprising of a large room and platform. Entry was free and proceedings were presided over by a verbose chairman who exhorted the customers to contribute their services.

The Whitebait Concert Rooms in St. Enoch's Wynd started out in 1857 as a free and easy before the tables were replaced by stalls in the body of the hall. Admission cost 6d (2½p) with a free refreshment or cigar thrown in for good measure. Credited with pioneering "girlie" shows with all female casts working behind a wire for their own safety, James Shearer managed the Whitebait until 1868 when his widow took over. John Muir, who was chairman and musical manager of the orchestra combining piano, violin, bass, flute, clarinet, cornet and drums, forewarned audiences that indiscriminate encoring would result in part of the programme being omitted. There is no record of the frequency with which this sanction was enforced until development of the railway system necessitated closure of the Whitebait in 1872.

In Dunlop Street, David Brown's miniature Royal Music Hall functioned for 34 years until shut down as a safety precaution in 1887. The 300 capacity Victoria Music Hall in Anderston's Jamieson Lane lasted for a year (1873), while the Albert Music Hall which formed the two upper storeys of a building with shops on the ground floor in Calton's Landressey Street, was destroyed by fire in January 1876 after only eighteen months. Around this time, Victorian concert saloons became obsolete. Electric numbers which correspond to that in the programme were displayed on the proscenium arch of purpose built music halls, rendering the role of chairman redundant.

Clog dancers, especially TOM W. ROYAL, were the men that mattered at the Alexandra Music Hall in Cowcaddens Street. Although fitted throughout with electric light, it lasted a mere seven months when adverse publicity forced its reversion to use as a public house with entertainment in May 1899.

Three months earlier the Tivoli had set forth on its short stuttering sojourn. Staffed and managed by many formerly associated with the Scotia Music Hall, the house at Anderston Cross had comic singers CHARLES COBURN, TOM HUGHES and MORNY CASH as turn of the century attractions. Renamed the Gaiety in 1907, it failed to last the course as a music hall and became Scotland's first licensed cinema in 1909.

EMPIRE

Arguably the best known Scottish music hall outside Glasgow, the Empire began life as the Gaiety on 30th March, 1874. Owner Charles Bernard had converted the Choral Hall at the corner of West Nile Street into a small theatre concentrating on Shakespearean and musical plays. Within three years, new proprietors conceded to public clamour for less serious offerings and introduced music hall. The London contingent that made their way to the Gaiety included MARIE LLOYD, GEORGE LASHWOOD of "Champagne Charlie" fame; coster comedian GUS ELEN, and TOM COSTELLO while the American comedian R. G. KNOWLES was there in 1895.

Off to a flying start, the landlords decided to rebuild and replace the Gaiety with the more grand and spacious Empire Palace. Appropriately on Burns Night 1896, the Gaiety went out in style with a celebration to the National Bard exactly 100 years after his death.

Designed by specialist theatre architect Frank Matcham in his customary opulent French Renaissance style at a cost of £30,000, it's first bill on 5th April, 1897 was topped by impersonator VESTA TILLEY. The task of whetting the Glasgwegians' insatiable appetite for high speed vaudeville was well served by the Moss family and resident manager for the greater part of two decades.

Closed in August 1930 to allow major internal reconstruction, a mammoth theatre with 2100 seats, four suites of rooms for the big brass and twenty dressing rooms on four floors emerged. The new Empire opened on 28th September 1931 with JACK PAYNE'S BAND; satirist BILLY BENNETT; and ventriloquist A. C. ASTOR as headliners accompanied by DR. HENRY FARMER'S pit orchestra. A brochure printed for the occasion described the decor as "restrained classic ornament, the colour motif is scrumbled ivory with sub-themes of plum and silver, and the draperies and upholstery are in Rose du Barry with silver satin appliqué work."

After Moss relinquished control, but not before the Glasgow Empire had earned it's reputation as the "English comics' graveyard", Bernard Leslie managed affairs for boss George Black of the London Palladium. While irreverent West of Scotland audiences found it difficult to rate English "funny men" as highly as they did themselves, it was a different story when the Americans jetted into the Empire in the fifties. Film-goers congregated to see their Hollywood idols in the flesh, and the rafters rang with appreciation of their observations of life and sharpness of wit. DEAN MARTIN & JERRY LEWIS; BUD ABBOT & LOU COSTELLO; STAN LAUREL & OLIVER HARDY; BOB HOPE; DANNY KAYE; JACK BENNY; DOROTHY LAMOUR; JUDY GARLAND; SOPHIE TUCKER; THE ANDREW SISTERS; FRANK SINATRA; and LIBERACE were but a few to make trans-Atlantic trips to the Glasgow Empire.

By March 1963, harsh economics decreed that the second largest variety theatre in Britain should be sacrificed for another soulless office development. Scotland's international house of variety is gone but certainly not forgotten!

ALHAMBRA

Sightseers thronged Waterloo Street on the night of 9th December, 1910 to eye the swagger evening dress crowd arriving in chauffeur driven limousines. Everybody who was anyone in Glasgow's social swim seemed to congregate at the site of the former Waterloo Rooms. The occasion was the opening of Glasgow's Alhambra Theatre.

Acknowledged as the best equipped theatre north of London, with a surfeit of technological gadgetry, it was the last word in comfort, refinement, acoustics and sightlines for the 2400 patrons relaxing in sumptuous seats. Whilst hesitating to classify this grand temple of the arts as a music hall, the first sixteen years saw international personalities of stage and radio making tracks to Glasgow's showpiece theatre for twice nightly variety. By the late twenties it was decided to utilise its considerable resources by staging opera, plays and musical comedies when the Alhambra attracted stars in the highest society of show business.

HARRY GORDON and WILL FYFFE teamed up in seven consecutive pantomimes for Tom Arnold before dapper minstrel ALEC FINLAY took over the role of principal comic for seventeen successive seasons. Lavish productions were the order of the evenings at the high brow Alhambra. Admission prices had been set with the more affluent in mind, a policy which continued after the Alhambra became part of the Howard & Wyndham empire in 1954.

"Five past Eight" revues with JACK RADCLIFFE and JIMMY LOGAN moved to the Alhambra running in tandem with a similar spectacle at the Edinburgh Kings. Equal in appeal was the Fol-de-Rols, a cascade of song, dance and comedy in the best possible taste. A highlight of these were the antics of DENNY WILLIS whose knockabout routines and gyrations of his gangling frame transcended all ages. The partnerships of JACK MILROY and RIKKI FULTON also had a big say in the Alhambra's fortunes. Their stage and television portrayals of the likeable layabouts Francie and Josie won them the Scotland's Light Entertainers award in 1970.

Other distinctions for the Alhambra were the staging of Scotland's first Royal Variety Show on 3rd July 1958 when the well heeled parted with £50 for the best seats; the debut of the world renowned BLUEBELL DANCING GIRLS in May 1960 and presentation of the Scottish premiere of the "My Fair Lady" musical in May 1964.

Among the big names to register at the Alhambra during their various eras were HARRY LAUDER, SARAH BERNHARDT, NORMAN WISDOM, GRACIE FIELDS, TOMMY HANDLEY, ARTHUR ASKEY, DAVID NIXON, CYRIL FLETCHER, BETTY GRABLE, MIKE YARWOOD, MAX BYGRAVES, BRUCE FORSYTH, WINIFRED ATTWELL and LESLIE CROWTHER.

In spite of a public clamour for its retention, CILLA BLACK and the unenviable role of presiding over its final curtain in May 1969. Yet another mundane office block rose in its stead.

BRITANNIA MUSIC HALL

Founded as Campbell's music saloon in the Trongate, it sprang to life as the Britannia Music Hall under the eagle eye of Albert Hubner. Many of the British, Irish and American luminaries of the Victorian music hall appeared at the "Brit" which was one of the few halls to feature cinematography before the end of the nineteenth century. Counter attractions at new custom built music halls forced its closure in 1903.

After lying dormant for three years it was used as a museum and waxworks by the colourful Bradford eccentric Albert Pickard, proprietor of the Clydebank Gaiety. Renamed Panopticon, the amusement complex ran four shows daily with tattooed and bearded ladies, midgets, strongmen, funfair sideshows and a menagerie.

A section of the Panopticon was then turned into a miniature music hall in which the audience stood, while the ladies' orchestra, which accompanied the turns, had the only seats in the primitive surroundings! Maintaining the Britannia tradition of Friday "Amateur Nights", the manager stood in the wings equipped with a long pole. The crook at its end was placed round the neck of aspirants who didn't come up to scratch. They were unceremoniously yanked off the stage before suffering the further indignity of a pelting with rotten fruit from the hyper-critical onlookers. Two who came through this ordeal unscathed were Helensburgh born JACK BUCHANAN of musical comedy fame and a boyish STAN JEFFERSON (later STAN LAUREL) who related jokes and comic songs heard whilst on duty at his father's Metropole in nearby Stockwell Street. Known as the Tron Cinema for four years from 1923, when it reverted to its familiar title of Panopticon, until closure in 1938.

Now occupied by leather retailers, the Britannia survives as Scotland's earliest (1857) music hall. Behind the debased lime painted Italianate facade, superficial alterations have been made to the two storeys above the shop. Sadly neglected, the floors which housed the auditorium and dressing rooms retain the proscenium arch and horse shoe shaped gallery beneath a roof in a sorry state of disrepair.

COLISEUM

Designed by the distinguished theatre architect Frank Matcham for Moss Empires Ltd., the Coliseum in Eglinton Street opened its doors on 18th December, 1905. A mammoth undertaking in which the Matcham manner was seen at its exhuberant best, it sat 2893 with standing room for another 318.

For many Glaswegians on the South Side, the Coliseum provided the first glimpse of the enthralling world of live theatre. Twice nightly music hall with pantomime over the festive season was the format at the Coliseum as at most of the theatres in the Moss network. Magicians, conjurors and illusionists resplendent in formal attire or flamboyant costumes cast their spell at Glasgow's Coliseum. Among these wonderworkers of yesteryear, THE GREAT CARMO made a lion vanish and "Handcuff King" HOUDINI proved equal to every challenge.

It was DR. WALFORD BODIE, however who made the greatest impact. A superb illusionist and ventriloquist with a mania for publicity, he was continually at odds with the medical profession in the course of his hypnotic and bloodless surgery. The misappropriation of the "M.D." tag after his name (BODIE contended that the initials stood for "Merry Devil") didn't endear him to the men of medicine whose hostility surfaced at the Coliseum. Barracked by students, BODIE responded by casting aspersions quoting Burns to the effect that "they gang in stirks and come oot asses". This barb was too much for the sensitive under-graduates who returned on the Thursday to pelt BODIE and his cast with eggs. The fall of the curtain failed to deter the infuriated academics who stormed the stage undeterred even by a police presence which had joined the fray. This clash at the Glasgow Coliseum on the 12th November, 1909 was enshrined in local folk lore as the "Bodie Riot".

Principal boy in many Coliseum pantomimes was FLORRIE FORDE. Her forte was the hearty singing of songs with catchy choruses and her fame is linked with "Down at the Olde Bull and Bush" and "Pack up your troubles" which were the vogue during and after the Great War. Soft shoe shuffler G. H. ELLIOTT and comedians BILLY MERSON, JOCK MILLS and SAM THOMSON were other favourites.

By 1929 the Coliseum had outlived its usefulness. Its elephantine proportions and remoteness from the city centre hastened its demise as a viable theatre. On conversion to a cinema, the interior was totally transformed with the balcony and gallery, which had consisted of tiers of concrete surmounted by wood and no backs, replaced by one tier. Although the exterior is basically unaltered, modifications and appendages added over the years have done little to enhance the Edwardian variety palace.

EMPRESS PLAYHOUSE

November 1987 was a sad month in the annals of Scotland's music hall history when the gaunt sandstone walls of the former Empress on St. George's Road were reduced to rubble. With little consideration given to its value as a local resource, it was forfeited for the construction of luxury flats. Its end rendered the Pavilion the only traditional music hall left in a city which boasted five theatres devoted wholly or in part to variety thirty years ago.

Opened with Edwardian bravura as the 1125 seater West End Playouse for operatic productions on 4th August, 1913, it fell on hard times within six months. Sails trimmed, it was relaunched as the Empress Variety Theatre and Picture Playhouse on 30th March, 1914 under Harry Godwin. In its early days Empress programmes had a strong Irish and American influence with a slot allotted for the American bioscope, the forerunner of Hollywood movies.

Taken over by George Urie Scott in 1933 with Jimmy Nelson as manager, the Empress concentrated on the provision of twice nightly variety. Grand old man of Scottish show business, GEORGE CLARKSON, first appeared in a double dance act with his son at the Empress in 1934 — one of the many helped to fame in this nursery of talent. Patrons frequently saw budding stars at the red plush and gold ornamented Empress, unknowns at the start of their careers who became big names in the world of entertainment.

The list of Auld Lang Syne comics is long and distinguished, with the Empress embracing many seasons with the droll CHARLIE KEMBLE. He had a penchant for playing unpredictable tricks and reeling off impromptu verses about regulars in the audience and locals in the public eye. PETE MARTIN, who first came to the notice of the public as a straight man to CHARLIE HOLBEIN, played countless Empress winter shows. Teaming up with JIMMY LANG latterly, his tuneful whistling and fine tenor voice were given full rein. The prodigious talents of ALY WILSON; BILLY RUSK and JOHNNY BEATTIE were manifest in their shows at St. George's Cross throughout the 1950s.

Having enjoyed a singular immunity from fire for over forty years, the Empress met the customary fate of so many theatres in September 1956. The ceiling was subsequently renewed and the gallery modified by the formation of a lime box with a seating capacity reduced to 120 on three tiers of timber steps. A large wardrobe room was located at the rear of the gallery. Constructed on a pillarless design, the circle sat 445 plus two boxes for 24 and standing room for 55. There were uninterrupted views of the 23 foot by 67 foot stage from 697 tip up stall seats. Sold to the Falcon Trust for £32,500 in February, 1960, as part of a scheme to present serious productions, the change of title to Falcon Theatre failed to bring a change in fortunes, and it folded under financial difficulties within two years.

Alec Frutin, erstwhile proprietor of the Stockwell Street Metropole, stepped in, renaming it New Metropole. The curtain rose again on twice nightly variety on 15th November 1962, with "Scotland Calling". Typical of these tartan spectaculars was the 1963/64 winter show produced by Danny Regan in which top draws CLARK & MURRAY were supported by soubrette BETTY MELVILLE; soprano RAE GORDON; vivacious dancer IRENE CAMPBELL; tenor DENNIS CLANCY; accordionist ARTHUR SPINK; THE ALEXANDER BROTHERS; duetists GEORGE CORMACK & IRENE SHARP; the JOE GORDON FOLK FOUR and the BRAEMAR LADIES PIPE BAND.

A saviour in the person of JIMMY LOGAN paid £85,000 for the music hall at the gate to the West End in 1964. Under his ownership the New Metropole had several box office successes, most notably was the American tribal love rock musical "Hair" with its nudity and oaths. Seen

by over 200,000 patrons within six months, its headline catching run of
38 weeks ended on 28th March, 1971. Thwarted by officialdom in his attempts to develop the New Metropole into a premiere show spot incor-
porating a licensed restaurant, Jimmy Logan put up the shutters in 1972.
Ironically, his customary role of topping the bill at theatres throughout
Scotland had been reversed at the Metropole where footing the bill became
an unacceptable burden.

GRAND THEATRE

Not entirely a new theatre, the Grand was a refurbished Prince of
Wales Theatre which had dated from 1867. Situated in the midst of the
densely populated Cowcaddens, the stage door and main entrance faced
Wiliam Street with access to the pit and the gallery gained from Stewart
Street. When the Grand surfaced on 19th September 1881, it sat 2030 with
standing room for another 165 in the three storey auditorium.

The Grand maintained the tradition for drama and pantomime set
by the Prince of Wales until fire intervened on 5th September, 1918. Only
a portion of the pit and the tenement frontage remained intact, and it was
rebuilt as the New Grand Picture House in 1920 only to be bulldozed for
a stretch of roadway half a century later.

LYCEUM

When it opened in November, 1899, the Lyceum was Glasgow's
biggest theatre. Built for Rich Waldon who already owned the Royal
Princess and Palace theatres in the Gorbals, it had room for 2300 seated
and 700 standing patrons. Animated pictures were on the scene when electric lighting was installed in 1904, but it was seldom utilised to the full.

Opera, musical comedies and drama, with which the Lyceum was first
associated, lost favour and were replaced with music hall in 1912. The
distaff side was well represented with FLORRIE FORDE; MARIE
KENDALL and LILY MORRIS making random calls to Govan's centre
of entertainment. A big event in the Lyceum's history was the appearance
of actor JOHN LAWSON who toured Britain and America extensively
with his "Humanity" music hall sketch.

The excellent acoustics were used to good effect when talkies arrived
in 1929, and the switch to movies was irretrievable three years later when
the auditorium was enlarged. Fire ravaged on 24th October, 1937, it was
recommissioned as a mecca for cinema goers. Bingo was introduced in

1974 and, after functioning as a dual entertainment complex for seven years the Lyceum went over exclusively to bingo.

METROPOLE

Fourteen months short of its centenary, the Metropole was Scotland's oldest music hall when it went on fire on 28th October, 1961. A smouldering shadow of its former self with the roof, circle and gallery destroyed, it was never revived. An integral part of Glasgow life for countless families vanished with its loss.

Built on the site of a joiner's yard at the rear of a public house in Stockwell Street, it emerged as the Scotia Music Hall on 29th December, 1862. James Bayliss was the prime mover behind the project. His widow Christina assumed the boss' mantle on his death and booked many of the old time favourites including the GREAT VANCE; MARIE LOFTUS; W. F. FRAME; VESTA TILLEY and CHARLES COBURN. The Scotia also provided HARRY LAUDER with his first professional opportunity from which he never looked back, going on to receive the accolade of music hall's first knight.

In 1893 Messrs. Thornton, Kirk and Moss became proprietors, the latter transferring his affections to his new Sauchiehall Street Empire four years later. This defection coincided with the transformation of the Scotia into a playhouse with the name Metropole, specialising in blood curdling melodrama. At the turn of the century the Metropole came under the direction of Arthur Jefferson whose son Stanley helped in minor parts when not truanting at the Britannia Music Hall in the Trongate. As STAN LAUREL the thin doleful half of the film clowns LAUREL & HARDY he spent most of his Hollywood days refining the craft first expressed at Glasgow's Metropole and Britannia.

Music hall returned when ownership transferred to Bernard Frutin in 1926 — a policy pursued with equal vigour and effect by sons Hyman and Alec until the fateful fire. The limited size and proportions of the Metropole helped to create personal artiste/audience relationships and the whiff of the old Scotia music hall was seldom absent in its cramped dressing rooms, stage and auditorium. The Metropole never pretended to cater for the elite or gentry but provided fun, glamour and excitement for families packed into tenements on both sides of the Clyde. Inhabited by all age groups, mothers with weans in shawls wrapped about their bodies were a familiar sight in the gallery. A real family atmosphere prevailed with bags of sweets passed freely across the tight squat rows of seats.

Closely associated with the Metropole were Jack and May Short who presided over long summer revues. Parents of comedian actor and impressario JIMMY LOGAN and jazz singer ANNIE ROSS, their Logan Family Shows in which Erin's Queen of Swing, EILEEN CLARE, and champion dancers JESSON & FARRELLY were prominent, enjoyed a loyal following for the best part of twenty years. Another favourite at the Metropole was the very personification of the people on the other side of the footlights, TOMMY MORGAN whose pantomimes often played until Easter to crowded houses. Tartan spectaculars with GRACE CLARK & COLIN MURRAY and JIMMY CURRIE'S real waterfalls and dancing fountains also drew variety buffs to the Met in the heady 1950s.

Many Scottish comedians and singers who went on to fame and fortune had beaten a path to the Stockwell Street music hall for their first big chance. They are unlikely to forget the debt owed to the venue which as the Scotia and Metropole, had not been scorned by LAUDER, LAUREL and LOGAN.

OLYMPIA THEATRE

Fitted out with cinema apparatus from its inception on 18th September, 1911, the proprietors had little faith in the Olympia's long term prospects as a music hall. Their misgivings were realised in 1924 when the powerful medium of the screen took its toll. The worthy reversion to live entertainment never materialised and for the next fifty years it was known as the ABC at Bridgeton Cross.

It had all been so different when the red sandstone building surmounted by a balcony received its hansel. Press reports of the day tell us that the accommodation of 2000 seats was taxed to its capacity at both 7pm and 9pm houses. The intricate plaster work and interior scheme of decoration of white and gold was admired by patrons who paid 2/6 (12p) for a seat in the private boxes; 1/6 (7½p) for the orchestra stalls; 1/- (5p) in the circle; 6d (2½p) in the pit, and 3d (1p) in the gallery. These charges spoke volumes about the social divisions of the Edwardian age. The premium rate admitted one of the privileged to upholstered fauteuils by way of foyers replete with every convenience. The same money allowed twelve impoverished souls to be penned in the pit or shunted up dimly-lit stone stairs, with a halt at the miniscule pay-box, to benches in a gallery with few facilities.

Poor and rich alike appreciated actor violinist JAN RUDENYI; illusionist CARMO; the wirewalking and musical troupe of THE FIVE WHITELEYS; wandering violinist RINALDO; and CORBIN and his dogs in early bills booked by Sam Lloyd. Fellow director and showman Harry McKelvie crossed the Clyde to give his theatrical expertise to his Royal Princess's when the Olympia stopped functioning as a Theatre of Varieties.

PALACE THEATRE

The building next door to the Royal Princess Theatre in the Gorbal's Main Street was known as the Grand National Halls at the turn of the century. Recreated as a music hall by Bertie Crewe, who had seen his magnificent Pavilion Theatre of Varieties hanselled in Renfield Street a fortnight earlier, it opened as the Palace Theatre on 14th March, 1904. With two houses at 7pm and 9pm, the Palace was the recognised place to foregather for families on the Clyde's south side. Replete with every comfort and convenience, with a whiff of the extravagant, the Palace welcomed celebrities of the music hall including baritone DAVID FULLER; Cockney comedian LEW LAKE; light comedian FRED BARNES; Scots comedians JOCK MILLS and NEIL KENYON; jolly little Dutch girl MAY MOORE-DUPREZ; Singers ELLA RETFORD and LOTTIE LENNOX and DR. WALFORD BODIE. He chose the Palace in June 1913, to make his first reappearance at a Glasgow theatre after his confrontation with the medical fraternity at the nearby Coliseum nearly four years earlier.

In September 1914, owner Rich Waldon leased the Palace to Walter Thomson's picture house syndicate. Although programmes were divided between films and variety acts, the portents for music hall were not good and the silver screen dominated from 1930 until 1962 when bingo took over. Demolished in 1977, the Palace could have been cherished as part of the city's theatrical and architectural heritage. Thankfully, the prized plasterwork was salvaged and preserved for future generations by the vigilant curators of, appropriately, the People's Palace Museum.

PAVILION

Defying all the odds, Glasgow's Pavilion regularly purveys variety to this day. All the more remarkable as it is completely unsubsidised and receives no funding from the Scottish Arts Council and kindred bodies whose thoughts and cash are directed at higher cultural activities. It remains the last stronghold of a long music hall tradition in Europe's City of

Culture owing everything to a dedicated staff and patrons and nothing
to the public purse.

With its imposing terra cotta facade, the Pavilion Theatre of Varieties
was designed by Bertie Crewe in the grand manner for Thomas Barrasford.
The domed ceiling was surmounted by an electrically controlled sliding
roof for ventilation. Fine Rococo plasterwork on the circle, balcony and
box fronts; decoration executed in pure Louis XV; handsome mahogany
woodwork and the marble mosaic floor all lent the 1800 seat theatre an
aura of splendour.

No less amusing than the dentist advertising in the Pavilion programme "painless extractions with nitrous oxide for 4/- (20p) or cocaine
for 1/- (5p)", were the press observations on the "fashionable company"
which attended the Pavilion's first house on 29th February, 1904. We learn
that "among the elite there was quite a preponderance of ladies and
gentlemen of quality in evening dress". Alas, class consciousness and
respectability were all in Edwardian Britain!

All the eminent music hall worthies turned up at the Pavilion at some
time or other, none more so than FLORRIE FORDE. A strong pantomime
tradition was established in the 'thirties with HARRY GORDON and
DAVE WILLIS alternately playing eight weeks at the Pavilion before moving east to the Theatre Royal in Edinburgh. The 'forties and 'fifties saw
pantomime runs of sixteen weeks for JACK ANTHONY (with BERTHA
RICARDO and BOND ROWELL) and lengthy summer shows for
TOMMY MORGAN (with TOMMY YORKE; JIMMY HILL and
MARGARET MILNE). Bridgeton-born, bluff, big hearted TOMMY
MORGAN enjoyed a cult status from fans who readily identified with
his no frills approach to comedy. On his death in 1961 it was revealed
that he had asked that his ashes be scattered on the Pavilion's roof. His
ghost is said to haunt the Pavilion to this day.

These happy and hilarious summer seasons were emulated during the
1960s and early 1970s by LEX McLEAN (with JIMMY CARR &
VONNIE; RON DALE, and MARGO BENTLEY). Plentiful belly laughs
were assured when the master of timing with his clever one liners and asides
was the central figure. Another regular crowd puller to Renfield Street
was JACK MILROY with his clean infectious humour, seen at its best
in the Pavilion's Diamond Jubilee "World of Widow Cranky" adven-
ture in pantomime with CHARLIE SIM and SALLY LOGAN.

LULU from Dennistoun (real name Marie Lawrie) broke box office
records in 1975 with her irrepressible vitality and joyous personality.

BILLY CONNOLLY, HECTOR NICOL, GLEN DALY, FREDDIE STARR and ANDY CAMERON portrayed their own distinctive brands of humour while Scottish songstresses LENA ZAVARONI, SHEENA EASTON, LENA MARTELL and BARBARA DICKSON also scored heavily with Pavilion audiences.

It was anything but plain sailing for the Pavilion and there was gloomy speculation of closure after incurring heavy financial losses in 1981. Spared the fate which befell the Queens, Metropole, Empire, Alhambra and Empress Theatres, the 80 years old Pavilion was rescued by James Glasgow and transformed into a modest profit maker. Smash-hit shows with SYDNEY DEVINE; spells from hypnotist ROBERT HALPERN; pantomime with DENNY WILLIS, and one night gigs from the foremost modern television entertainers have kept the cash tills registering.

The Pavilion also plays a major role in the annual Mayfest — Glasgow's International Festival of popular theatre, music, the arts and community programmes. Little altered and virtually unspoilt since its inception, the seating capacity of 1449 is made up of 677 stalls, 341 circle, 413 balcony and 18 box seats. While the stiff shirts in chauffeur-driven cabs have given way to coach parties from the rural areas of Strathclyde and beyond, a policy of providing the best in live entertainment has been pursued consistently. The portents look good for the vibrant Pavilion Theatre of Varieties.

QUEEN'S THEATRE

No recollection of the palmy days of Scotland's music halls would be complete without paying tribute to the Glasgow institution that was the Queen's Theatre.

Colourful posters for the New Star Theatre of Varieties in 1885 proclaimed programmes "specially organised for the working classes". The Gallowgate music hall was "the only place of amusement in Glasgow that studies the welfare, comfort and pocket of the working classes by giving them only the very best talent, an extra strong band, gorgeous scenery at reasonable prices which are never changed." The modest admission charges fixed by Dundee proprietor Dan McKay were — Orchestra stalls (cushioned) 6d (2½p). First Circle and Pit 3d (1p); Gallery 2d (½p).

Formed out of the upper floors of a four storey warehouse block in Watson Street, it emerged as the Star Music Hall in 1878 and became the Shakespeare Music Hall three years later. Within six weeks of the name of New Star Theatre of Varieties being bestowed disaster struck on 1st

November, 1884. A false alarm of fire caused panic in which fourteen patrons were trampled to death in the ensuing stampede for the exits. Re-opened on 28th November, 1892 by Tom Colquhoun and Barney Armstrong as the Peoples Palace with JOE LANTY doubling as assistant manager and a comedian, it seated 2300 with standing room for 320.

The ultimate change of title to Queen's took effect from December 1897 when Fred Cooke ruled the roost. Bought by Glasgow Corporation for £15,000 in 1902, capacity was reduced to 1800 sat in stalls, circle and gallery with very basic accommodation and amenities for artistes and customers. Presentation varied between bawdy music hall and transpontine drama. Command performances were the Queen's stock-in-trade. Not very royal but full of variety!

Bills were presented twice nightly by itinerant comedians, singers, dancers, acrobats, jugglers, illusionists, magicians and novelty acts. The predictable drawing room frivolities of the more "respectable" theatres were no match for the uninhibited and earthy humour purveyed at the Queen's — an unlikely meeting place for the faint hearted, although legend has it that the braver members of the social elite ventured to see what amused the proteleteriat and were occasionally won over themselves by the experience.

Prior to the outbreak of the Hitler War and throughout the 1940s the Queen's played host to a series of ribald inelegant pantomimes. The scripts were written in the broadest Glasgow dialect by FRANK DROY who also appeared in a multitude of roles in the comedy scenes. Main pillars of those salty pantomimes were his wife contralto DORIS DROY, and SAM MURRAY who, irrespective of the subject of the panto-mime, invariably appeared as a dame called Fanny Cartwright. High on lung power and with an abundance of funny material, these cheerful pro-ductions epitomised the spirit of Glasgow.

Managed by Harry Hall for 22 years until 1951, the Queen's operated as a music hall with a distinctively Scottish flavour. JACK MILROY and CHARLIE SIM were two of the many who got their first professional breaks on its tough platform.

Fire put paid to it all on 24th January, 1952 when the dressing rooms, stage and ceiling were irreparably destroyed. Thirty artistes and musicians had lost their jobs, while the loss of this emporium of fun to the community near Glasgow Cross could never be quantified.

Whitebait Concert Rooms,

ST ENOCH'S WYND AND LANE.

General Manager, ... Mr GEORGE E. ADAMS
Musical Manager and Chairman, ... Mr JOHN MUIR

Leader of Band, Mr GRANT		*Flute*, ...	Mr PACKER
Pianist, ... Mr H. MAY		*Clarion* ...	Mr J. WILSON
Violin Secundo, Mr RAYMOND		*Cornet*, ...	Mr M'DOUGALL
Contra Bass ... Mr STUART		*Drums*, ..	Master HAYS

☞ Should indiscriminate encoring be persisted in, part of this programme must necessarily be omitted.

PROGRAMME FOR THIS EVENING.

Song, ...Miss LEIGHTON

Irish Comic Song,

MR O'GRADY

Serio-Comic Song, ... Miss EMILY CARR

Irish Comic Song,

MR FARRISEY

Serio-Comic Song,

MISS BRADLEY

Negro Entertainment,

BROS. EDWARDS

Serio-Comic Song,

MISS LEIGHTON

Irish Comic Duet,

MR & MRS O'GRADY

Character Song,

MISS EMILY CARR

Negro Entertainment,

HERMAN & ELSTON

Violin Solo,

MISS RIES

Wizard and Ventriloqual Entertainment,

PROFESSOR DUVAL

Serio-Comic Song, ... Miss BRADLEY

1857 - 1872

I

RENEE & BILLIE HOUSTON — 1934

GRACE and COLIN
CLARK MURRAY

"MR & MRS GLASGOW"

1945 — "VICTORY CELEBRATION"

THE BEST OF SCOTCH — Left to right: Jimmy Neil, Denny Willis, Tommy Morgan, Dave Willis.

BRITANNIA

PROGRAMME

THEATRE of VARIETIES

GLASGOW

Lessee and Manager, - - Mr. A. HUBNER.

MONDAY, FEBRUARY 1st, 1897. AND EVERY EVENING DURING THE WEEK.

1. Overture by the Band.

2. A. C. COWIE.
   Scotch Patter Comedian.

3. GOODWIN & HASPER.
   Statue Dancers, Banjoists and Knockabouts.

4. NELLIE BOLTON.
   Charming Serio Burlesque Actress.

5. DIDIE GODFREY.
   Mimic and Comic Troupe of Performing Dogs.

6. DIAMOND & STANLEY.
   Comedy Artistes and Speciality Dancers.

7. Selection.

8. N. C. BOSTOCK.
   The Comic King.

9. BENSON & BRADIE.
   Eccentric Actors, Patter Vocalists, and Dancers.

10. ARTHUR LESTER.
    The Popular Actor Vocalist.

11. National Anthem.

AMATEUR NIGHT EVERY FRIDAY.

Doors Open at 7, Overture at 7.30. Saturdays One Hour Earlier.
PRICES OF ADMISSION.
Body of Hall, 3d; Pit Stalls (Cushioned), 4d; Gallery, 4d; Circle, 6d;
Orchestra Chairs, 1s. Saturday and Holidays—Body of Hall, 4d;
Pit Stalls, 6d; Gallery, 6d; Circle, 9d; Orchestra Chairs, 1s.
The Management reserve the right to refuse admission to any person.
Pass-Out Checks, 1d each.
This Programme is subject to Alteration. Price ONE PENNY.

THE METROPOLE THEATRE, Stockwell Street, Glasgow
Saturday, 18th December, 1954

.·. T H E .·.

THEATRE

Proprietors:
Victoria Circuit Ltd.

PAISLEY

Manager:
Fred Luker.

| **6-45** | Commencing MONDAY, 30th OCT., 1950
T W I C E   N I G H T L Y | **8-45** |

New Resident Show! — For a Short Season!!

LAUGHING ROOM ONLY

★ ★ FEATURING SCOTLAND'S STAR COMEDIAN ★ ★
DIRECT FROM HIS BIG SUCCESS AT THE PALACE THEATRE, DUNDEE

LEX McLEAN

Harry **REDPATH**	Rita **CARDIE**
GIBSON SISTERS	Johnny **WHYTE**
CARR & VONNIE	
Billy **DUNLOP**	Moxon Ladies
BILLY GEORGE TRIO	**GIBSON** AND **SISTERS** BUDDY

COMPLETE CHANGE OF PROGRAMME WEEKLY

POPULAR PRICES OF ADMISSION

Booking Office Open Daily from 10 a.m. till 9 p.m.   Phone: Paisley 2025

VIII

ROYAL PRINCESS THEATRE

Her Majesty's Theatre near Gorbals Cross came to grief within six months of opening on 28th December, 1878. Renamed the Royal Princess by Harcourt Beryl, it presented a varied diet of music hall, melodrama and plays — a policy maintained by Beryl's former assistant Rich Waldon when he took over the reins in 1888. Of the many Scottish plays given regular airings in the 1440 seater Princess, few made a sharper impression on the national identity of Glaswegians than "Rob Roy". Concurrently a succession of British vaudevillians delighted Princess audiences in the hey day of music hall. Crowded houses were the order of the evenings in March 1909 for ELLA RETFORD'S Benefit. Her bell-like voice carried to the gallery, from whence a spluttering carbon-arc lamp spotlighted the artistes on stage. And never a microphone in sight!

Former page boy Harry McKelvie inherited the Royal Princess in 1922 and set out to establish it as the acknowledged home of prestigious pantomime in Glasgow. High in production values with colourful costumes and settings, the pantomimes were first written by Waldon and later by McKelvie. With the exception of the villain and principal boy, the cast were predominantly Scottish. TOMMY LORNE and POWER & BENDON had seasons before GEORGE WEST made his debut in 1924. Frequently partnered by JEANETTE ADIE and JACK RAYMOND, GEORGE WEST with his outlandish outfits and absurd facial expressions, reigned supreme in Princess' pantomimes for 21 consecutive years — a world stage record! Attended by young and old alike, all sections of Glasgow society took up the Princess' pantomimes with unbridled enthusiasm. Each show ran from late November until early June when the theatre closed until the next panto opened frequently preceded by a variety bill. They were never emulated for scale of production or for length of season.

In September 1946 the Royal Princess became the Citizen's Theatre under favourable terms of lease granted by Harry McKelvie. Shorn of its frontage with the distinctive statues in 1979 along with the adjacent Palace Theatre, the fabric of the old Princess survives as the 800 seater home of drama for the Glasgow Citizen's Theatre Company.

SAVOY MUSIC HALL

Readily recognised with its pair of towers and advertised as "Glasgow's Cosmopolitan House", the Savoy never made the grade as a first class music hall. After an encouraging start on 18th December, 1911 when American comedienne NELLA WEBB topped the bill, it was downhill all the way for live entertainment. Altered as the New Savoy cinema within five years, it showed films until March 1958.

Converted into the Majestic ballroom complete with Louis XVI decor and tea room adjoining the circle, bandleader DAVE MASON drew dance conscious Glaswegians to the Hope Street venue for thirteen years. Demolished in 1972 the site of the former music hall and cinema is now occupied by a shopping centre with the fitting name of Savoy.

Chapter
Two

"Paisley Pranks"

Paisley

Paisley

Prior to the construction of Mr. Brickwell's theatre in 1890, theatre in Paisley had occupied various premises of a temporary character. Performances were given at Highlet's hayloft near Seedhill Bridge to which patrons had access by an outside wooden stair, and the ballroom of the Tontine Inn was fitted up as the Bank Street Theatre. The Abercorn Street playhouse was superceded by the Royalty at Abercorn Bridge, and the Exchange Rooms in Moss Street were used as a theatre for strolling players before being renamed Theatre Royal and concetrating on music hall entertainment.

Designed by the London architects Bertie Crewe and W. Sprague, the Paisley Theatre had the distinction of being the first fireproof theatre built outside London. What had not been envisaged was the need to place duck boards in the dressing rooms. When the river Cart was in spate, water would lap the floors at the rear of the theatre and insidious fungi could be seen growing on the ceiling corners.

Accommodating 1200, the dress circle had sixty tip-up upholstered seats, the orchestra stalls 101 and the upper circle 120. The impecunious masses were left to stand or settle on wooden forms. Opened by the Paul Jones Opera Company on 25th October 1890, the Smithhills Street venue was the centre of Paisley's theatrical activity for seventy years.

Among the many English variety artistes guesting at the Paisley Theatre was "Britain's Prime Minister of Mirth" GEORGE ROBEY, later knighted for his services to music hall. At this time, policy and the purse strings were in the hands of a Mr. Saville. In 1921, control passed to the Scottish Central Theatre Company who operated the New Century Theatre in Motherwell, Hamilton Hippodrome, Falkirk Grand and Stirling Alhambra. Many itinerant revue companies stopped off for a week at Paisley were the clog dancing patter comic Brothers Hannaway presented "Posh", and Harry Kemp gave the Buddies editions of "Laughin' Gas", "Scotch Broth" and "Joy Express".

The Victoria Circuit became lessees in 1934, an arrangement which prevailed until the Wm. Galt agency ran the hall in its latter years as the Victory Theatre. Seasons of variety and repertory were interspersed by Fred Luker, the man in charge of day-to-day affairs. Typical wartime summer productions by Alec Ascot featured IKE FREEDMAN, Hebrew Prophet; yodelling cowboy ARCHIE ROY; singers MURIEL CRANSHAW and JACKSON MANLEY; and comedians TOMMY HOPE and JIMMY LANG. The orchestra was directed by Jimmy Burns.

Serving his apprenticeship in theatre administration after the war was JIMMY LOGAN. Before attaining top billing status as a comedy actor, he participated with his relatives in their annual Paisley seasons. A sure indication of their appeal was the opening of the normally unoccupied gallery for the redoubtable Jack Short's productions of the LOGAN FAMILY.

"Smiles in Smithhills" was an apt slogan for the annual ten week road shows headed by BILLY RUSK. The Bellshill comic with the pawky humour enjoyed a strong following with the townsfolk of Paisley. In the same category were pantomist GEORGE WEST; and the comedy teams of JIMMY DONOGHUE & JIMMY RAMSEY; RENEE HOUSTON & DONALD STEWART; and JACK MILROY & MARY LEE.

By 1957 variety shows were often limited to two houses on Friday and Saturday and it came as no surprise when the Victory Theatre closed on 10th January 1959 after a "Cinderella" pantomime. The building was razed when Smithhills Street was redeveloped in 1967.

In his verse "Paisley's Auld Theatre" local poet Thomas Barbour recalls the Smithhills house with the lines:—

> Gone are the days o' pit an' stalls,
> New fashions, picture, TV thrills,
> Nae mair we'll hear the curtain calls,
> In Saville's doon in auld Smithhills.
>
> Ye Paisley folks who read this page,
> May think the present greater,
> For me I'll dwell on 'prentice age,
> And Paisley's auld Theatre.

Chapter Three

"Land o' Burns"

Ayr

Dumfries

Kilmarnock

Ayr

GAIETY

The true story of this much loved theatre unfolds in October 1925 when it became the property of Ben Popplewell, lessee of the nearby Pavilion Theatre. Prior to that, the Gaiety had first operated from 1902 as a playhouse and latterly as a cinema. Neither venture had been fruitful.

All this was to change with the arrival of the Bradfordian impressario. After an extensive overhaul and scheme of decoration with blue and orange-amber the dominant colours, the new Gaiety emerged from the Depression to stage variety, revue and musicals. In next to no time, well known troupers were brought to the 1000 seater Carrick Street house whose fortunes were transformed. "Run by a family for all families" was the clarion call adopted by the proprietors. The name of Popplewell became synonymous with live entertainment at its best in the land of Burns.

Credited with setting the precedent for numerically big summertime shows in Scotland, their first resident revue in 1930 was a prototype for the famous "Whirls" which still have the crowds flocking from far afield. Main merrymakers in these fast moving revues were, in turn, DAVE WILLIS; JACK ANTHONY; ALY WILSON; JACK MILROY; BILLY RUSK and JOHNNY BEATTIE. With his clean subtle humour, catchy songs and clever impersonations, the resourceful and unselfish JOHNNY BEATTIE has worked tirelessly to keep the spirit of music hall alive in Scotland. It is a mark of the esteem in which he is held by promoters and public that he was given the signal honour of piloting this years 60th Gaiety Whirl. Supporting acts to make lasting impressions over the years include local baritone ALISTAIR McHARG; the musical comedy stars of "Oklahoma" and "Brigadoon" GWEN OVERTON and CLIVE STOCK; MARGO HENDERSON and SAM KEMP with music, song and impressions; STAN STENNETT with his zany brand of music and comedy; soprano and actress DOROTHY PAUL; and the dancing duos of RONALD BOWYER & JEANNE RAVEL and TERRY & DORIC KENDALL.

Most "Whirl" programmes comprise of three full scale musical scenes with concerted singing and dancing, when the singers give forth, often in unfamiliar roles, while the soubrette and dancers take steps to entertain. The first half invariably concludes with one of these sumptuously attired sets. Beauty of movement and form is evident when the second half gets under way with a troupe of chorus girls who supply grace, sparkle and precision dancing. This normally precedes spots for the accordionist and/or xylophonist, singers, novelty items, musical and dance speciality acts. The industrious comic will have done "cross overs" on the front cloth with his confederate while the scenery was rearranged; been the central character in sketches, and presented songs with patter and a character study before a grand finale in which the whole cast bid farewell.

The run of Gaiety Whirls was halted temporarily in August 1955 when fire damaged the roof and stage. Eric and Leslie Popplewell, who had taken control on their father's death five years earlier, sanctioned the restoration. A restyled modern Gaiety with reduced seating capacity of 570 and improved sightlines surfaced on 2nd July 1956 with the 27th Whirl.

Bought by Glasgow Pavilion Theatre Ltd., for £65,000 in March 1965, the close association of the two variety houses resulted in attractions being switched at both venues. CLARK & MURRAY; ALASDAIR GILLIES; KENNETH McKELLAR; ANDY STEWART and HECTOR NICOL fronted their own shows with unflagging zeal and no little success.

A demolition threat was averted in 1972 when it was taken over by the Town Council for £72,000. This coincided with the end of Harry Broad's forty years stint as the Gaiety musical director. Administered as a civic theatre in the Popplewell tradition, the Gaiety continues to provide the best available live entertainment for the family, as the flagship of Scottish Variety.

Revered by patrons, press and the many variety artistes it catapulted to greater heights, Ayr Gaiety has created a unique niche for itself in the history of Scotland's music halls.

PAVILION THEATRE

After the customary reservations had been expressed on its need and desirability, the municipal authorities parted with £8000 to build the Pavilion Theatre. Seating 1500 with standing room for another 900, it opened on 23rd May 1911. Promenades encircled the long narrow auditorium at both ground floor and balcony levels.

Impressario Ben Popplewell took over the lease from a beleaguered council in 1913. For the next twenty years a steady stream of eminent vaudevillians converged on the Esplanade music hall with Scotland's greatest character comedian, WILL FYFFE, in the vanguard on nine different occasions. FLORRIE FORDE was another regular, as were FRED KARNOS' Gangs and miracle worker DR. WALFORD BODIE.

HARRY TATE with his "Motoring" sketch; NELLIE WALLACE; GERTIE GITANA; RANDOLPH SUTTON; DOROTHY WARD and LUCAS & McSHANE (alias Old Mother Riley and her daughter Kitty) were a few of the big names to come to the "House that rocks with laughter" at the edge of the Low Green.

Charlie Kemble's Entertainers held sway at the Pavilion for four successive summer seasons from 1926 when a young song and dance man called JACK ANTHONY got a start "in the business". Comedians PETE MARTIN & CHARLIE HOLBEIN; TOMMY MORGAN; and finally WULLIE LINDSAY in 1933 led summer concert parties. Variety in the town of honest men and bonnie lasses was then concentrated at the Gaiety with the Pavilion becoming a rendezvous for trippers of the light fantastic.

From 1956 jazz sessions brought a succession of internationally known groups to the Pavilion. These included IAN MENZIE'S CLYDE VALLEY STOMPERS; BRUCE TURNER'S JUMP BAND; MICK MULLIGAN'S BAND with GEORGE MELLEY; JOHNNY DUNCAN AND HIS BLUE GRASS BOYS; SID PHILLIPS AND HIS ORCHESTRA; NAT GONELLA AND HIS GEORGIANS; DICK CHARLESWORTH AND HIS CITY GENTS; KENNY BALL'S JAZZMEN; ACKER BILK AND HIS PARAMOUNT MEN; HUMPHREY LYTTELTON, and CHRIS BARBER.

After an association with the Pavilion stretching over half a century, the Popplewell family relinquished the lease in 1967. The big band sound continues to boom as lovers of the terpsichorean art go through their intricate steps and gyrations on the maplewood floor.

With its 30ft. stage, acanthus leaf decorated proscenium, fine acoustics, distinctive horse-shoe gallery and theatrical ambience, the Pavilion's potential for full scale productions has been acknowledged. A recent variety bill headed by Irish cabaret crooner BRENDAN SHINE was a sell-out and hopefully a foretaste of more stage presentations in this old music hall.

Dumfries

LYCEUM

A masterpiece of design by Glasgow architect George Boswell, the Lyceum Theatre opened its doors in December 1912. A local enterprise, the directors of the Dumfries Theatre Company were restaurateur Robert Oughton, bank agent George Russell and solicitor Mathew McKerrow.

Access to the 1500 seats was obtained via a glass-covered porch which lead to a large vestibule out of which doors to all parts of the building opened. Three double doors gave access to the auditorium while on one side a wide staircase lead to the circle. The floor of the auditorium swept down to the proscenium and was covered with crimson velvet tip-up pit and stalls chairs. The mahogany woodwork and plasterwork of different shades of grey made an effective scheme of decorations. A portion of the floor in front of the narrow stage was sunk to accommodate the three-piece orchestra.

Many first class travelling dramatic, musical comedy and revue companies stopped off at the Lyceum which also enjoyed its fair share of opera from the Moodie-Manners and Allington Charsley Companies. The latter was the world's largest Grand Opera Company when over a hundred artists and orchestra descended on the Queen of the South in March 1919 for the 94th consecutive week of their tour. HARRY LAUDER, WILL FYFFE, CHARLIE KEMBLE and DAVE BRUCE were a few of the luminaries in variety and pantomime at the original Lyceum before its demolition in May 1936.

Five months later the new Lyceum was erected on the site of its predecessor at the south end of the High Street. Architect of the new complex which cost £25,000 was Alister MacDonald, son of Britain's first Labour Prime Minister. The need for corridors was eliminated with the entrance foyer leading directly to the stalls foyer at each end of which stairways took you to the circle from whence another staircase without balustrades lead to the balcony. A grandson of actress ELLEN TERRY, Edward Carrick, painted cartoons on walls of the balcony foyer depicting a series of amusing aspects of people and life. Longer by 35ft and wider by 76ft than the old Lyceum, the new theatre sat 2000 when full. A spacious orchestra pit fronted the 44ft wide proscenium which was flanked by clustered columns in gold. Incorporated in a room off the stairways between the stalls and balcony foyers was a cafe for those seeking sustenance.

Doubling as a cinema and theatre, the Lyceum presented orchestral concerts, plays by National and amateur companies, variety programmes and films of the day. Eminent violinists who gave concerts were TOSCHA SIEDEL and ALFREDO CAMPOLI from London's Grosvenor Hotel.

Yet another theatre and palatial edifice was lost to commercial development in January 1970! But not before DAVE WILLIS, TOMMY MORGAN, JIMMY LOGAN, ANDY STEWART, baritone BILL McCUE, the CORRIES FOLK GROUP, the ALEXANDER BROTHERS, and bare-footed songstress SANDIE SHAW had done their best to keep variety alive in Galloway.

Kilmarnock

The first straight theatre in Kilmarnock was the Opera House which started in 1875 from its base in John Finnie Street. Its days were numbered, however, as access to the bigger temples in Glasgow became easier and devotees of drama forsook the Operetta. It was converted into a church in 1885 and saw several uses including that of an auction saleroom before housing discotheques and bars in a contemporary "Nitespot". Gutted by fire in April 1989 and internally a total loss, there are hopes of preserving the front of the three storey listed building.

KINGS THEATRE

Built of red sandstone at a cost of £19,000 on a site between Tichfield Street and St. Andrew Street, the imposing Kings Theatre accommodated 2200 in pit, stalls, eight boxes, family circle and gallery. The 50ft by 32ft stage had a proscenium opening of 28ft.

The Kings opened on 3rd October 1904 and counted MARTIN HARVEY; FRANK BENSON and EDWARD COMPTON among its early players. In spite of the lavish praise heaped on the Kings by COMPTON who "did not recall so handsome a temple of Thespis in a similar sized town or in most towns of twice Kilmarnock's population" it did not prevent the company who owned the playhouse going into liquidation in 1908. It was acquired by John Cummings, lessee of the Corn Exchange the following year. Among the eminent British music hall stars he brought to the Kings were FRED KARNO; ALEX LOFTUS; CHARLIE KEMBLE; HARRY GORDON; ALFRED DENVILLE; and HARRY LAUDER.

From 1925 silent films were introduced and the "talkies", which arrived four years later complemented the variety shows until April 1934 when the Kings became a cinema. The interior was gutted leaving only the outer walls of Alex. Cullen's original construction. Renamed the Regal in 1939, it became the ABC Cinema in 1964. The lower storey was then converted into a bingo hall and social club in 1973 and a triple screen complex incorporated in the main hall in 1976.

PALACE THEATRE

BILLY CONNOLLY cut the tape at the launching ceremony of the renovated Palace Theatre on 31st August 1985. With its new auditorium for 500, new foyer and bars, 25ft square stage and orchestra pit for up to sixteen musicians, it was the ultimate in computerised technology. The occasion marked a fresh era in the theatre's chequered career, for chequered it assuredly had been! The building with the classical Victorian red sandstone exterior which we now know as the Palace Theatre started as the town's Corn Exchange in 1863 at a cost of £6000. It was not until 1903 that it was converted to a music hall with a fully equipped stage.

Under the judicious management of John Cummings the Palace of Varieties furnished the best of music hall with its spontaneity and bawdy, earthy entertainment. FRED KARNO'S Company, which fostered CHARLIE CHAPLIN; LITTLE TICH with the galvanic legs; and chorus singer FLORRIE FORDE were early arrivals. In a Scottish context, minstrel W. F. FRAME; hypnotist and illusionist DR. WALFORD BODIE; and tenor J. M. HAMILTON kept the saltire flying. WILL FYFFE got £7 for his week as second comedian in the 1915 "Risk It" revue, and RENEE & BILLIE HOUSTON were also set on the upward path at the Kilmarnock Palace. In common with many music halls, the Palace adapted to changing tastes in the thirties by showing films. The alternation of pictures and music hall turns was the vogue until both brands of entertainment were put on separate weeks.

Abortive attempts were made to make the Palace a civic theatre in 1948 when it was known as the Exchange Theatre, but even the presence of DUNCAN MACRAE and MOLLY URQUHART did not prevent a succession of closures. Run by William Cummings, son of the theatre's first lessee, the Palace staged repertory, variety, pantomime and drama for four years. Names which adorned the doors of the Palace dressing rooms in the forties and fifties included TOM F. MOSS, the Carl Rosa Opera tenor; ROBERT WILSON; WEE GEORGIE WOOD; TOMMY HOOD; SAMMY MURRAY; VAL DOONICAN (then with the RAMBLERS), and OSCAR RABIN and his Band.

Kilmarnock Arts Council had a brief spell in control before fire intervened in 1979. The District Council then spent £190,000 on repairs and refurbishment, and a smaller modern Palace Theatre was launched in September 1982 with a variety show in which comedian JOHNNY BEATTIE; duetists JOE GORDON & SALLY LOGAN; and singer ANNE FIELDS reaped the plaudits. Few weekends now pass without offerings of music, song and comedy by the Palace of Variety. Shows fronted by KEN GOODWIN; ALAN PRICE, and THE CORRIES and the annual pantomime are but a few of the more recent attractions at the former Corn Exchange.

In narrating the story of Kilmarnock's Palace it would be churlish not to mention the efforts of those working behind the scenes. This band of unsung heroes was typified by the Kennaugh family. In his capacities as call boy, lime operator and stage electrician, Tom ensured that the show went on, while father James worked at the Palace and Aberdeen Tivoli theatres as a scenic artist. Roller fitted back cloths were readily lowered and lifted for quick scene changes in smaller theatres with limited stage depth. These frequently formed the main part of the scenery varying from household and street scenes to landscaped gardens with trees and hills rolling into infinity. Examined at close quarters the finished articles were a mere assortment of colour and it was only when viewed from a distance that the paintings took shape into identifiable scenes.

Chapter Four

"Pickard Unlimited"

Clydebank

Clydebank

Clydebank's first purpose built theatre was the New Gaiety. Located in Elgin Street at the corner of Glasgow Road, it sat 1400 in orchestra stalls, pit, dress circle and upper circle. Dramatic plays were produced after its inauguaration on 29th January 1902, but these received a mixed response and gave way to musical plays and music hall. Friday Amateur contests invited comic and sentimental singers, clog dancers, Highland dancers, cake walkers, musicians, Irish and Scottish comedians, song and dance couples and tug-of-war teams to compete for handsome prizes. Concessionary prices to the pit were withdrawn on Friday — a measure of the appeal of these "open to all comers" nights.

The Gaiety came under the direction of the flamboyant eccentric Albert Ernest Pickard on 14th September 1908. A shrewd and colourful character, Pickard first caught the headlines as owner of the Panopticon Theatre and neighbouring museum and wax works in Glasgow's Trongate. Styling himself as "A. E. Pickard Unlimited of London, Paris, Moscow and Bannockburn", the little dynamo went on to establish a chain of cinemas and properties throughout the West of Scotland. Never slow to sing his own praises, Pickard proclaimed that he was known throughout the Empire for his cinematograph pictures. These were duly introduced at Clydebank's Gaiety where NORA SULLIVAN and her troupe of lady athletes and wrestlers; WINONA, champion lady aerial shot of the world; the BROTHERS FERGUSON, midget champions in wooden shoes; and ALF WARNER novelty musician and raconteur were but a few of the Gaiety turns under Pickard's regime. The theatre closed on 9th June 1917 with the appropriately named "Cheerio" revue by the Albany Company. It re-opened as a picture palace eight weeks later, became the Bank Cinema in November 1927 and closed for good on 30th September 1961.

Dating from 1908, Cinema Varieties in Graham Street was a corrugated building with twin towers comprising a small hall and tea room. The seats and private boxes were all on one level. Bioscopes were included in the early music hall programmes. Renamed the Palace in December 1915, the emphasis had swung to pictures before it sustained considerable bomb damage during the 1941 Clydebank blitz.

EMPIRE

Amid the celebrations on Hogmanay 1914 the pleasure seeking citizens of Clydebank took time to attend the opening of the Empire in Glasgow

Road. The electrically lit theatre with seating for 800 in the stalls and circle and 500 in the gallery staged music hall before switching to pictures in 1927. Headliners at the Empire were — ELROY the armless wonder whose feet performed the actions usually delegated to the hands; CORA CORINA, quick change artiste; ERNESTO, comedy musical equilibrist; G. W. FYVIE, Irish comedian and expert dancer; LENA & LEWIS, the black and white comedy due, and the LEVAINES in patter and harmony at the piano. The Empire was destroyed by fire on 21st June 1959.

PAVILION

The fourth addition to Clydebank's pleasure palaces opened on 29th December 1919. The Pavilion was built on the roomy and airy amphitheatre-like principle favoured in America and the elliptical form of construction enhanced the acoustic properties of the house which accommodated any kind of theatrical production on its 30 square foot stage. The 2000 oak seats were made by disabled soldiers. The moving force behind the Pavilion Picture and Variety Theatre was George Urie Scott who controlled many theatres and cinemas in Glagow, and was credited as the innovator of the arrangement whereby jam jars were accepted "in lieu" to gain entry to his premises.

On entering the Pavilion at Kilbowie Road, patrons had a clear path to all parts with stalls seat holders on leaving the vestibule passing through an underground passage below the theatre to gain their seats. Clydebank's big wigs attended the grand opening when dancing club juggler PAULINE MARS and the troupe of FIVE JOCKS headlined. From the outset, silent pictures were displayed in addition to music hall, pantomime, drama and plays. It was wired for sound in 1931 when the talking movies were introduced. Born within sight of the Pavilion, ALEXANDER McLEAN CAMERON (alias LEX McLEAN) made his professional debut at the theatre as pianist in the pit orchestra. He went on to enrapture variety theatre audiences as Scotland's uncrowned king of comedy until his death in 1975.

Many a deserving relief fund and institution benefited from Pavilion concerts before the best efforts of the Fire Service failed to subdue the flames which engulfed the building on 8th October 1942.

Chapter Five

"*Clyde Coast*"

Greenock

Gourock

Dunoon

Rothesay

Largs

Greenock

No less a worthy than James Moss, father of Edward who was to found the circuit of Moss Empires, introduced music hall to Greenock in 1873. An itinerant diorama presenter and singer of comic and character songs, he rented the Mechanics' Institute in Sir Michael Street. Alliterations abounded in his publicity ploys, typified in the claim that James Moss would introduce mirth making merry musical morsels for melancholy moments and mimics of men and manners. A strong Irish influence was brought to bear in his Royal Lorne Music Hall promotions in which clog dancers complemented comedians and singers. This affinity with the Emerlad Isle was to manifest itself in many of the Greenock Empire shows long after the Moss family had departed.

KINGS THEATRE

Built at the corner of Ker Street and Grey Place in 1905, the Alexandra accommodated 1900. It had ten private boxes, pit and orchestra stalls on ground level, family and dress circles on the first tier, and amphitheatre and gallery on the second tier. The dome which capped the circular tower was a prominent landmark from most parts of the town and river. Local control and management was assumed by Messrs Alec and John Wright whose father had long been associated with the Theatre Royal. Although the emphasis was on grand opera, drama, plays and farces; vaudevillians also had their say in the persons of male impersonator HETTY KING, comedy card manipulator CARLTON, chorus singer LOTTIE LENNOX and an exclusive engagement in April 1908 of the GREAT LAFAYETTE; the self-styled illusionist.

Designated the Kings in 1910, it remained the home of legitimate drama with the OSMOND TEARLE; EDWARD COMPTON; GEORGE EDWARDES and CARL ROSA OPERA COMPANIES frequent visitors. Local amateur productions were given every encouragement and facility by the Wrights until Bostock took over in August 1926. Variety and plays were then presented at a time when the Depression and unemployment had taken a toll on the hardy Clydeside citizens. After a four months repertory season the Friedman family acquired and converted the Kings into a cinema in August 1928. A pioneer talkie house from March 1937, it made a brief return to stage productions during the war when a number of shows were produced for servicemen in the district.

When subsequently bought by the Rank Organisation in September

1955, the boxes and stage were stripped away, dressing rooms removed and the auditorium extended in the redesignated Odeon. The interior bore little resemblance to the original Alexandra Theatre when it was lost for all time in 1973 under a compulsory purchase order.

HIPPODROME

Dating from 1858, the Theatre Royal in West Blackhall Street provided legitimate drama for half a century before it was superceded by the Alexandra. It was remodelled, reseated and redecorated to emerge on 28th August, 1905 as the Palace Music Hall with CAPTAIN WOODWARD'S SEALS the top attraction. The Palace had a brief foray as the Pavilion before being retitled Hippodrome under the direction of Harry Skivington.

It may have seemed ironic that a building with niches flaunting statues of Shakespeare and other thespian characters housed such diverse entertainment as the ADRIAN TROUPE in bicycle pursuit racing on a 9ft diameter track angled at 75 degrees; SEARS the American illusionist; Greenock comedian NEIL KENYON; descriptive singer GEORGE LASHWOOD; and J. L. SULLIVAN who delivered his inimitable monologue before giving a three round exhibition of self defence with JAKE KILRAIN.

The Hippodrome closed in December 1923 and was obliterated from Greenock's busiest thoroughfare in May 1930 under an improvement order.

EMPIRE

The hanselling of the Empire Theatre in Manse Lane on 16th March, 1903 was greeted with hype in full measure. Bills proclaimed "that all classes were delighted and that every artiste was applauded to the echo". There were no waits or old fashioned kill-time acts with every artiste performing their best business in half the usual time taken up in old music hall style shows. The inaugral programme which created such a stir comprised of a Scottish ventriloquist from London; an American comedy duo; a unique juggler; three dancing marvels; the finest lady tumbler in Europe; a mimic; a comedy sketch, and four electrical musical artistes.

From these dizzy heights, the Empire established itself as the recognised hall of vaudeville for two generations of Greenockians. It received amongst others, the VYPONDS as Society entertainers; BENYON, world champion cyclist, and LILY MARNEY the gem of Irish comediennes before being renovated in August 1906. HARRY TATE, renowned for his sporting sketches; the ELLIOTT SAVONAS, trick cyclists and saxophonists; WILKIE BARD'S COY, and in other realm MAURICE DE RIAZ champion wrestler of Switzerland came to the Manse Lane house before the B.B. Picture Coy secured the lease in March 1910.

The era of pictures and speciality acts lasted until 1926 when full time twice nightly variety was reinstated. Advertisements for the Empire read "Tis not in mortals to command success, but we'll do more — deserve it!" Living up to these expectations were wonder man MORRITT; magician, CLIVE MASKELYNE; PINDER'S CIRCUS; O'REILLY'S VAUDEVILLIANS; and comedians ELLIS DRAKE and CHARLIE KEMBLE. Lesser lights were frequently subjected to a tirade of abuse, and it was not uncommon for wire netting to be placed around the orchestra as protection against rivets hurled by disillusioned shipyard workers.

Ownership of Greenock's last commercial theatre passed to David and George Wooley in 1933. The proven format of variety and revue artistes foregathering for a week at the Greenock Empire before moving to fresh pastures in a new combination survived the Hitler war years to be replaced by touring road shows. These were topped by Scottish and Irish personalities such as the LOGANS; DONOGHUE & RAMSEY; CECIL SHERIDAN; DENNY WILLIS and the unique comic genius that was Greenock-born CHIC MURRAY.

Heavy expenditure in alterations and the provision of a licensed bar in 1954 failed to halt the decline in attendances and the 920 seats were seldom fully occupied. After a spate of summer closures and abbreviated engagements with two houses restricted to Friday and Saturday, the Empire staged its last professional performance on 14th May, 1957. Sold to the Corporation the following year, the Empire was used as a furniture store and auction room for a further ten years before demolition in October 1968, to make way for the city centre redevelopment project.

ARGYLE THEATRE

Originally St. Michael's Church in Argyle Street, a new music hall with 1000 tip-up seats was opened on 1st October, 1928.

Advertised as "Greenock's Cosy Corner", ELLIS DRAKE and JACK RAYMOND started proceedings with ARTHUR HAYNES the parody king and DR. WALFORD BODIE other early attractions.

Licensed in turn as a theatre and boxing arena, the pugilists made way for the Mechanics Institute whose Tobago Street premises were blitzed in 1941. Successively an amusement hall, shopping arcade and discotheque, the stage and stalls are now occupied by pool tables in a leisure complex. Furniture is displayed in the balcony, and artifacts stored in the supposedly haunted basement dressing rooms.

Gourock

While the Empire faded into oblivion, Greenockians in search of live entertainment took the short trip to the Cragburn Pavilion. From May 1936 this all-purpose venue staged summer shows in which Scottish and Irish artistes featured in Pete Davis' productions of Alec Finlay's Frolics.

With variety on the wane during the 1970s, it was left to the thinning ranks of troupers who had learnt their craft on the arduous music hall circuit to keep the business vibrant. Few were better qualified to meet this task than compere, comic and singer GLEN DALY. Programmes in which "MR GLASGOW" was anchorman bristled with a wealth of fun, song and music.

Reduced in circumstances, the Cragburn Pavilion now hosts community activities, dances and the occasional amateur stage production.

Largs

BARRFIELDS PAVILION

Taking its name from benefactor Robert Barr, Barrfields Pavilion was formally opened by his widow on 11th April, 1929. Equipped with a full size stage, 1000 seats, dance floor and tea rooms, its first season was a financial disaster.

A reduction in rent for the second lessee brought improved results. Harry Kemp, who staged six week summer concerts in his Saltcoats La Scala cinema, was impressario at Largs during the thirties. Prominent in his "Sunny Days" revues were comedians GEORGE WEST and BERT DENVER along with singers SYLVIA CECIL; ROBERT NAYLOR; DONALD PEERS and a lass destined for musical comedy stardom, PAT KIRKWOOD.

Commandeered during the war as a repair base for sea-planes, it was 1948 before revues returned to Barrfields. With the exception of the summers of 1950 and 1951 when bandleader LOUIS FREEMAN had the lease, theatrical agent George Bowie was awarded the lets until 1974.

The auditorium was enhanced in 1955 with the installation of 740 permanent seats. These were all occupied more often than not when ALEC FINLAY; GRACE CLARK & COLIN MURRAY; and the Irish song and patter brothers JOE and DAVE O'DUFFY were in lively Largs. A camaraderie between artistes and audience was evident in revues which were full of spirited dancing, homely humour and delightful songs.

In common with other Clyde resorts Largs felt the draught when holidaymakers flew out to warmer climes. The 1960s saw a format of one nightly house in June and September with two in the holiday boom months of July and August. This led to abbreviated seasons of weekend shows in which, among others, baritone PETER MORRISON sang arias and duets from opera and musicals to appreciative audiences. The stall seats were removed in 1980 when a cinema room was built to the leisure centre that is now Barrfields Pavilion.

Dunoon

Summer seasons of variety were an integral element in holiday packages offered from 1905 at the Pavilion in Castle Gardens until fire took its toll in April, 1949. A multi-purpose building of contemporary design seating 1200 in the main hall and 285 in the balcony opened on 25th April, 1958 as the Queens Hall in Pier Road.

Cowal Carnivals were typical seaside shows with casts of fifteen giving their best on the 50ft by 30ft stage. The basic format was similar to that of more elaborate productions with songs, sketches, dancing and musical items offered individually and in different combinations. For reasons best known to themselves, these end-of-pier type shows were deemed more socially acceptable to a section of the public who gave the same entertainment a wide berth when presented in its familiar setting of a city music hall.

Visitors had good reason to be glad of the comfort and bright varied fare within the walls of the compact Cosy Corner from 1945 until 1957. Comedians FREDDIE SALES; DENNY WILLIS and BILLY STUTT participated in holiday revels there before gaining prominence on television, while singers who forsook the gainful environs of London for Dunoon included BILLIE ANTHONY; DONALD PEERS and ISSY BONN.

Of the many lights of the variety stage who frequented Dunoon, few made a greater impact than JIMMY NEIL with his "A'm Next" catchphrase and warm spontaneous humour. Equally at home as a compere, front cloth comic and singer, he had a penchant for listing innumerable song titles in renditions of amusing airs. His like will not be seen again!

Rothesay
WINTER GARDENS

Affectionately known as the Madiera of Scotland, the Isle of Bute has welcomed visitors to her shores for centuries. Few Glaswegians haven't savoured a trip "doon the watter" on the "Waverley" paddle steamer to Rothesay at the heart of the Firth of Clyde. For those arriving by sea at the ferry terminal, the principal landmark is the Winter Gardens Pavilion.

Built as a music hall in 1924 for £7000, an earlier bandstand was incorporated in the structure. Of an unusual style with its art nouveau ironwork, corner towers and tiled pagoda roof, the Winter Gardens' spacious interior has a system of iron beams encompassing the domed hall.

Lessees of the 1200 seat hall for over twenty years were Fyffe and Fyffe, when Gordon Inglis' "Rothesay Entertainers" provided the requisite sparkle and cheerfulness for summer visitors. The 1950s found Fraser Neal as lessee when the far-travelled "Cock of the North" PETER SINCLAIR; jolly rotund PETE MARTIN; character comedian JIMMY REID; master of repartee DON ARROL and the foremost Scottish variety acts of the day were attractions. The Rothesay Entertainers, with local accordionist ELLA WILSON often to the fore, provided varied musical and humorous fare until 1971 when declining tourist trade brought weekend summer shows to an end.

Moves are afoot to make the vacant Winter Gardens a maritime heritage centre with facilities for small stage productions. Architectural bodies have weighed in to the rescue plan, backed by music hall buffs who remember a seaside lifestyle unlikely to return to the pride of Bute.

Chapter
Six

"Capital Capers"

Edinburgh

Edinburgh

Music hall began in the capital in 1861 when stockbroker Wm. Paterson took over the Dunedin Hall. He transformed the structure which had housed circuses into the Alhambra Music Hall, but within a year the property was deemed unsafe and closed. Undeterred at this rebuff, Paterson opened his new Alhambra on the opposite side of Nicolson Street. Renamed Royal Princess, it failed to pay its way and petered out in 1886 to be revived as the La Scala cinema in 1912. Along the road, Charles Hengler literally folded his tent to house the Southminster Music Hall as a circus in 1863. Gutted by fire in 1875, it was rebuilt as the Queens Theatre with J. B. Howard, who was to found the Howard & Wyndham theatrical enterprises, in control until 1880 when James Newsomes' Hippodrome and Circus emerged on the site destined to house Britain's first Empire Theatre twelve years later.

Adam House at 5 Chambers Street was the location of the Gaiety Music Hall in 1875. The hall with a reputation for risque fare was leased by Herbert Moss who bought adjacent shops and the University Hotel above the theatre. Artistes on the Moss circuit, most journeying from London halls, certainly earned their corn, having to put on an extra turn at the Kirkgate Hall every Saturday. Horse drawn cabs whisked them to Leith after completing their twice nightly routine at the Gaiety. On moving round the corner to his first Empire in 1892, Moss closed the Gaiety, which was retitled the Operetta House presenting cine-variety before going over to films exclusively.

Down town in St. Stephens Street, the 2000 seater Tivoli opened in November 1901. Stockbridge hostelries made much of their close proximity to the new music hall in advertisements which highlighted the fact that they were equipped with an electric bell which would ring two minutes before the curtain rose for each act. Within three years, the name had changed to Grand and its transition to cinema finally effected by 1920. As Tiffany's in the 1960's and 1970's it welcomed cabaret stars like singer MATT MUNRO. Altered beyond recognition from its music hall days the short lived Tivoli now functions as Cinderella Rockerfellas nightclub.

Within a year of HARRY LAUDER'S birth at nearby Bridge Street in 1870, Portobello pier was contructed complete with a concert party pavilion at its terminus, a familiar landmark between Bath Street and Wellington Street for 45 years. In 1907 Harry Marvello inaugurated the Tower Pavilion on the promenade with his Geisha Entertainers, one of Portobello's many live attractions.

Dubbed the "Brighton of the North", Portobello was a mecca for holiday makers between the wars. While Jimmie Whitelaws' pierrots made for the Palace, summer shows were housed in the Bath Street Pavilion by Andre Letta. His succinct message was:—

"Let us go to Letta's Show
Where talent holds the sway,
If you haven't paid a visit yet
There's a million Scots wha hae".

EMPIRE PALACE

Described as "the most gorgeous man-made place of entertainment in all Scotland" the forerunner of Edward Moss' thirty super theatres was built on the site of James Newsome's Hippodrome and circus in Nicolson Street. Designed by the doyen of theatre architects Frank Matcham, with seating for 2016, the Empire Palace opened on 7th November 1892. Entrance to the stalls and circle was by way of a corridor and staircase with marble mosaic floors, while the less favoured approached the hard benches in the gallery for the price of a groat from a pend off the Potterrow. A proportion of the large circus stage encroached on the auditorium and the moveable proscenium gave flexibility to run circuses or variety shows. A sliding roof provided extra ventilation.

The first programme taxed its resources to the limit with a confection of singers, comedians, performing cockatoos and dogs, a massed military band and an orchesta of thirty. Another first was recorded when moving pictures, "the greatest novelty of the age and latest scientific triumph", were seen for the first time in Scotland at the Edinburgh Empire on 13th April 1896.

The story of the capital's Empire is overshadowed by the GREAT LAFAYETTE disaster. Sigmund Neuberger left his Munich home for America in 1890 entering vaudeville as an archer and quick change artiste and taking out U.S. citizenship as LAFAYETTE. A superb showman with expert knowledge of stagecraft and colour displays, his specialities were large illusionary effects and spectacles. LAFAYETTE was paranoid about the welfare of a bull terrier gifted to him by HOUDINI. A gold collar encircled the neck of "Beauty" permanently. When the dog died five days after his opening engagement at the Empire, the illusionist had it embalmed and buried in Piershill cemetery stipulating that he would be interred in the same plot when his time came. This death wish was fulfilled with

GERTIE GITANA — "The Idol of the People" — 1926

LUCAN and McSHANE
OLD MOTHER RILEY FILM SERIES

LYCEUM THEATRE
& PICTURE HOUSE
High Street, DUMFRIES

Proprietors THE DUMFRIES THEATRE C LTD   Licensee&Manager, John R. Haddow.

ALL WEEK, commencing MONDAY, 25th MAY
SATURDAY AT 2.15, 6.15, AND 8.30.
Nightly at 7.30.   Early Doors, 6.50; Ordinary Doors, 7.10.

ENORMOUS ATTRACTION

HARRY KEMP
PRESENTS

SCOTCH
BROTH

A. Palatable and Pleasing Concoction in 14 Bowls, prepared and dished up by PETE DAVIS.

NAE 'GAULD KAIL HET AGAIN ABOOT OOR SCOTCH BROTH

FLORA   DALTON
MACDONALD & PAYNE
THE POPULAR COMEDY ENTERTAINERS

Maie Wynne	DESSIE	Jimmy
POPULAR CHORUS COMEDIENNE	DESMOND'S	Macdonald
JOHN WEST	PASADENA	LIGHT COMEDIAN
IRELAND'S EMINENT BARITONE	GIRLS	Billy Pethers
Edith M'Leod		THE MAN IN THE CHAIR
BRILLIANT SOPRANO		

PETE   DAVE
DAVIS | WILLIS
THE VERSATILE-ITE   THE NEW COMIC

Prices of Admission (Including Tax)
Front Stalls, 3s 6d; Stalls, 2s 4d; Pit Stalls, 1s 3d; Pit, 8d
Early Doors, 1s 0d; Early Doors, 1s.
Front Balcony, 3s 6d; Back Balcony, 1s 10d.

1925

AYR GAIETY GIRLS — 1929

MARGO HENDERSON & SAM KEMP

AYR GAIETY — 1989

CLYDEBANK

PAVILION

Proprietors THE CLYDEBANK PAVILION Ltd.   Manager—J. MARTIN

ONCE NIGHTLY at 7.30
6-45 SATURDAY—TWO PERFORMANCES 9

WEEK COMMENCING **MONDAY, 23rd FEBY., 1925**

FRED COLLINS PRODUCTIONS LTD.
PRESENT THEIR LATEST COMEDY REVUE

SAY
WHEN!
IN 10 DIFFERENT BLENDS

All-Star Caste, featuring the LATEST JAZZ SENSATION, THE

MANHATTAN MELODY MAKERS 9 IN NUMBER

Including NINETTE, the DEMON DRUMMER from the CAPITOL THEATRE, NEW YORK
In their Popular GRAMOPHONE SUCCESSES

LESTER & WOOD	KITTY EVELYN
FRED ANDERSON	ALEC FOSTER
A. E. MANN	MAE LANDOR

THE UKULELE GIRLS   THE SIX DANDY STEPPERS

ROYAL COURT JUVENILES
(TEN IN NUMBER)

FULL BEAUTY CHORUS
AUGMENTED ORCHESTRA under the direction of Mr JAMES RUMBERG

Scenery by   W GLOVER, Jr   Properties by   R O FLETCHER
Dresses by FRED COLLINS PRODUCTION DEPT. Glasgow and Edinburgh

Manager   FOR   A. L. SHAND
Stage Carpenter   FRED COLLINS   RICHARD ALLTREE
Wardrobe Mistress   PRODUCTIONS Ltd.   MIDGE, HALLETT

CHILDREN'S
PICTURE MATINEE
EVERY SATURDAY AT 2.30   BALCONY 2d: STALLS 1d

TERROR
A THRILLING PHOTO PLAY IN SIX PARTS, FEATURING
PEARL WHITE

PRICES OF ADMISSION:
FRONT CIRCLE   CIRCLE   STALLS   PIT.

1/3 Booked 1/6	1/- Booked 1/2	8d. Booked 1/-	5d.

ALL CHILDREN MUST BE PAID FOR.

XV

ROTHESAY ENTERTAINERS, SEASON 1925.

FRED DAVIS.   ROBERT MACHRAY.   CHARLIE KEMBLE.   HARRY MILLEN.
MONTY McVEAN.   DAISY CARR.   JULIAN ROSS.   MAY MILBY.   BIJOU GORDON.
HELEN CAMPBELL.   ELLA CARR.

XVI

uncanny alacrity on 9th May 1911 when the GREAT LAFAYETTE and nine of his retinue perished when fire engulfed the stage. Another sad consequence of this disaster was the loss of the first Royal Command Variety Show which had been scheduled for the Empire weeks later.

Business resumed on 7th August 1911 after the fire damaged quarters had been repaired. ALBERT CHEVALIER rendered "My Old Dutch"; the white-eyed kaffir, G. H. CHIRGWIN, played a one string fiddle and sang "I am but a poor blind boy"; VESTA TILLEY appeared as "the perfect gentleman"; HARRY HOUDINI escaped from his Chinese water torture cell; and the Australian dandy, ALBERT WHELAN, whistled his signature tune "The Jolly Brothers" while casually removing his coat, top hat, white scarf and gloves.

The Empire Palace was decommissioned for ten months from November 1927 when the promenades on either side were removed and the width of the building extended to 88ft. The structure on three floors of stalls, circle and balcony which emerged is the Empire with which we are familiar today. JACK BUCHANAN, the debonair light comedian of the top hat and tails brigade, invited his admirers to "Stand Up and Sing" when the big touring bands of the thirties were also Empire headliners.

The Hollywood comedy team of STAN LAUREL & OLIVER HARDY came to the Empire in 1954 around the same time as comedian TED RAY; trumpeter EDDIE CALVERT; and American crooner JOHNNY RAY, who had tearful teenagers screaming in the aisles. JACK RADCLIFFE, JACK ANTHONY, ROBERT WILSON and ANDY STEWART are only representative of the better known Scottish personalities who with their Companies provided laughter, song and dance for a generation. One of the main pillars of theatrical life in Edinburgh, the Empire staged its last live show on 27th November 1962. The bustle of burlesque gave way to the call of bingo on 6th March 1963 when Mecca paid £165,000 for the original Moss Empire.

Plans are supposedly well advanced for the City to buy the Empire, thus ending the seemingly interminable search for a Festival Theatre. This noble reversion of an under-utilised asset would be welcomed well beyond the boundaries of "Auld Reekie".

GARRICK THEATRE

Twice nightly music hall once echoed from the walls of the Garrick Theatre on the Grove Street site now occupied by Marco's Leisure Centre. Opened on Hogmanay 1917 by the former lessees of the Theatre Royal,

Edinburgh Varieties Ltd., offered the revue "Hullo Baby" as an appetiser. Prices were pitched at 1/10d (9p) for orchestra stalls; 1/3d (6p) for the circle, and 8d (3p) for pit stalls.

Posters beckoned the public to see "real natives" when THE HAWAIIANS and Mdlle. LEILAN introduced the original Hula Hula dance. Musical and comedy burlesque were the strong cards of the Haymarket house whose fare varied from J. M. Hamilton's Concert Party to the ATLAS VULCANA GIRLS displaying feats of strength. MARY CONNOLLY, the Dublin street singer, topped the Garrick's last programme when fire engulfed the building on 4th June 1921.

Prior to Horace Collins taking over the Garrick, it had operated under five different names. Started off as the New Pavilion Theatre on 15th February 1897, it became the Prince of Wales in January 1906, the Alhambra before the year was out and Pringle's Picture Palace (named after proprietor Ralph Pringle) in 1908.

KINGS THEATRE

Not readily identified as a music hall, the Kings has staged variety at fitful intervals since opening its doors in 1906. Built as a "House of Variety" under the scrutiny of Stewart Cruikshank, the Kings was a recognised number one touring venue, and as part of the Howard & Wyndham empire from 1928, was in the vanguard for revue, opera, drama, ballet and pantomime.

Extensive alterations in 1951 saw seating capacity reduced from 2500 to 1530 when the gallery and family circle were amalgamated. Ownership passed to the City in 1969, and after years of procrastination, a £1.25 million refurbishment scheme was approved in 1985. Behind the red Dumfriesshire sandstone facade, new upholstered seats for 1330 are approached by way of marble halls and staircases with art nouveau brasswork. An enlarged ten foot deep orchestra pit complete with hydraulic lift is the most imaginative addition to the Kings Theatre now restored to its pristine Edwardian grandeur.

Summer revues with DAVE WILLIS, "Five past Eight" shows with RIKKI FULTON & JACK MILROY; and pantomimes with HARRY GORDON, JIMMY LOGAN and STANLEY BAXTER enthralled generations of family audiences. International names who stalked the Kings stage include MARIA CALLAS; SEAN CONNERY; NOEL COWARD; WILL FYFFE; DOUGLAS FAIRBANKS; IVOR NOVELLO; TYRONE POWER; ANNA PAVLOVA; LAURENCE OLIVIER and PAUL ROBESON — a litany with which the Capital can be justifiably proud.

PALLADIUM

Two years short of its centenary, the Palladium vanished in 1984 when the demolishers wreaked havoc on the East Fountainbridge emporium of fun. Opened by John Henry Cooke as a circus in November 1886, the public discovered a ring encircling a sawdust-covered floor on which a show of juggling and equestrian acrobatics was given.

The Circus finished in 1911 and the Palladium was adapted to display silent films. The advent of sound movies required a fairly hefty investment to make smaller cinemas like the Palladium viable. The capital wasn't forthcoming and the cinema closed in August 1932. A benefactor came from a most unlikely quarter when Millicent Ward normally associated with the Gateway Theatre in Elm Row, kitted it out with a proper stage and dressing rooms and presented repertory there for three years.

From 11th April 1935 the Palladium was a home for variety and revue. Although it always had the look of a modified cinema on two floors, the atmosphere of music hall with its infectious bonhomie filled the 960 seater Palladium. Especially when the king of Scottish Showmen, LEX McLEAN was the focal figure. He often appeared during the Festival when the Palladium also staged late night Oxbridge-type revues with casts headed by DAVID FROST and his ilk. Lex took this in his stride proving that most people prefer a laugh to enlightenment. With invaluable assistance from JIMMY CARR & VONNIE, GLEN DALY and MARGO BENTLEY, Lex McLean created the record for the Palladium's longest period (25 weeks) of top box office returns.

Pedestrians and motorists held up at the Earl Grey Street traffic lights may ponder that a few yards away there stood a music hall were comedians DAVE BRUCE; JIMMY NICOL; ALEC FINLAY; DENNY WILLIS; JOHNNY VICTORY who did much good work for charitable causes, and the tall, droll and small doll team of CHIC MURRAY & MAIDIE trod its boards. Singers in national attire who brought a breath of the hills and heather to East Fountainbridge included ROBERT WILSON; COLIN STUART; DENNIS CLANCY; CALUM KENNEDY; KEN & ALAN HAYNES; GEORGE CORMACK & IRENE SHARP, and TOM & JACK ALEXANDER. Balladeers DONALD PEERS, RICHARD HARDIE, and JOHN & BETTY ROYLE struck the right chords as did crooners LARRY DAVIS; STEVE CAMERON; DANNY DRYSDALE (alias STREET) and local lad JACKIE DENNIS who appeared on American televison with PERRY COMO. Sopranos to catch the eye and ear included MAUREEN

KERSHAW; GRACE CALVERT; SHIELA PATON and RAE GOR-
DON. In the top rank of dance acts were the O'DOYLE BROTHERS
& JEAN; BILLY CAMERON & IRENE CAMPBELL; KATHLEEN
KEMP & EDDIE KEENE; the trio of BETTY BRIGHT; DESMOND
CARROLL and LINDSAY DOLAN; AL FULLER & JEANETTE; and
ROLAND ROY & JACKIE TOADUFF. The latter widened their appeal
by breaking through as a dynamic song and dance duo on cruise liners
and in cabaret while consolidating their roots on the variety stage. Also
remembered in the Palladium roll call are managers Dan Campbell and
Andrew Foley and the small band of pit musicians led by pianist Helen
Fowler.

Patronage fell when many of the Tollcross citizens moved to better housing on the outskirts of the city and the final curtain fell on the Palladium
in 1968. The building had a spell as a discotheque before demolishers swept
it into the rosy nostalgia of Scottish music hall lore in 1984. Happy Nights!

THEATRE ROYAL

Phoenix-like, the Theatre Royal rose from the ashes on four occasions before finally succumbing to fire on 30th March 1946. It was the
fifth theatre built at the junction of Leith Street and Broughton Street
and the fifth destroyed by fire. A descendant of a building in which circus,
concerts and plays had been presented, the establishment was known as
Corris Rooms, the Pantatheon, Caledonian, Adelphi and Queens Theatre
before being named Theatre Royal when the older theatre of the same
name made way for the General Post Office.

Acquired by Howard & Wyndham in 1896, it staged the first Edinburgh production of "Peter Pan" and enjoyed a great tradition in
pantomime. Many of the legends of music hall were seen within its walls
— saucy MARIE LLOYD; the cross talk double act of "Underneath the
Arches" fame, BUD FLANAGAN & CHESNEY ALLAN; JIMMY
NERVO & TEDDY KNOX of the "Crazy Gang"; character comedians
ROBB WILTON, G. S. MELVIN and the American musical comedy act
of FORSYTH SEAMON & FARRELL to name but a few.

Edinburgh Varieties Ltd. bought the Theatre Royal, and after
embodying many improvements, reopened in July 1935 with impressario
Horace Collins at the wheel. A succession of seasonal shows headed by
JACK ANTHONY; DAVE WILLIS; JACK RADCLIFFE and ALEC
FINLAY won a special niche in the regard of young and old. Also bring-
ing the crowds to the theatre at the top of Leith Walk were heavyweight

of the xylophone TEDDY BROWN; "laughing legs" MAX WALL; political jester and impersonator LESLIE STRANGE; raconteur JAMES HUNTER; stage and screen star JIMMY JAMES; illusionist CECIL LYLE; master of mystery DANTE; GRACIE FIELDS and husband ARCHIE PITT with "Mr. Tower of London"; eccentric sand dancers WILSON, KEPPEL & BETTY; BILLY RUSSELL joking on behalf of the working classes; adagio dancers GANJOU BROTHERS & JUANITA; and pianists CHARLIE KUNZ and TURNER LAYTON.

A character in his own right who managed the Royal was A. J. "Bumper" Wark. He presided in the halcyon days of variety and revue when theatres in the Collins' camp like the Aberdeen Tivoli and Glasgow Pavilion emulated the fare and comfort provided by the more fashionable but less inviting Stoll and Moss Circuits. Tommy Morgan and his Company had just completed their third week of "Hail Caledonia" when, within an hour of curtain-down, the Theatre Royal was yet again struck down, never to be rebuilt.

Chapter
Seven

"Leith Larks"

Leith

Leith

Before the Princess was established as Leith's first permanent theatre, four music halls had come and gone in short order. The Leith Royal Music Hall in St. Andrew Street set the trend in November 1865, to be followed by the Theatre Royal on the corner of Bonnington Road and Great Junction Street, managed by Alfred Macarte, a part-time pantomist and step dancer. Next on the scene was the New Star Music Hall at the corner of Duke Street and Leith Walk. The News Theatre sprang up in Bangour Street in March 1888 when a company of serio-comic vocalists and Irish and negro artistes were promised, but it was the largesse that hit the headlines. Every person entering the theatre had an equal opportunity of winning — gold and silver watches; beef and mutton, hams, sacks of flour or potatoes, pictures, melodeons and mirrors. In return for a shilling (5p) Leithers had the best seats in the house, or for a quarter of that outlay a view from the gallery with a gift token as a further inducement.

GAIETY

The Princess Theatre was opened by Edward Moss on 30th December, 1889, on the site of the old U.P. Church in the Kirkgate, but within ten years it was considered inadequate for housing the larger London productions. After reconstruction it reopened as the Gaiety on 30th October, 1899, under the control of Mr R. C. Buchanan, Moss having withdrawn to concentrate on his Empire Palace in Nicolson Street.

The new century was heralded with the special engagement of the Chalmers Cinematograph and grand installation of electric lights. At a time when the working man did well to earn 30/- (£1.50) for his week's work, HARRY HOUDINI received £200 for his two weeks engagement at the Gaiety. Having defied all his challengers when they brought their handcuffs, leg irons and other restraints, HOUDINI was carried shoulder high to Leith Central Station after the final performance on 8th July, 1905 to the strains of "Will Ye No Come Back Again?"

The theatre was enlarged in 1914 when shops on either side of the main entrance were transformed into additional facilities, changes which coincided with the programmes alternating between moving pictures and stage shows. The closely knit community of shipyard workers, dockers, whisky warehousemen and their families in the port identified with the Gaiety especially after the enforced amalgamation with Edinburgh in 1920.

Affectionately known as the "Gaff" with its "Go as you please" competitions on Friday, the Gaiety ran "a penny and red one" for advertisers
who were admitted for a penny on submitting the red pass.

Used intermittently as a cinema in the thirties, the Gaiety reverted
to full time variety on 3rd July, 1944 when TOMMY HOPE started the
proceedings. Leith Entertainers Ltd., appointed Claude Worth resident
manager in March 1946, and he lost no time in promoting shows led by
local funster ALY WILSON; BOBBY TELFORD; TOMMY HOOD;
JIMMY NEIL; DENNY WILLIS, and the LOGAN FAMILY. The Gaiety
also provided a springboard for young show business aspirants. In March
1953 an unknown ANDY STEWART, who climbed to the pinnacle in his
profession as a singer, songwriter and interpreter of Scottish character,
and DON ARROL, who went on to host television's "Sunday Night at
the London Palladium" made their professional debut. The Lex McLean
and Johnny Victory road shows were big draws at the Gaiety before it
closed in September 1956. It was demolished in May 1963, as part of the
Kirkgate slum clearance and redevelopment scheme.

ALHAMBRA

Leith's other theatre of consequence was the Alhambra situated at
the corner of Springfield Road and Leith Walk. It started life as a music
hall in December 1914, bringing the latest war pictures in its twice nightly
programmes to 1550 seat capacity audiences. The management made great
play of the grand orchestra of fifteen and of the theatre's close proximity
to the Pilrig and Leith Central Stations; which were destinations for companies headed by violinist MACKENZIE MURDOCH; singer
DURWARD LELY, and comedian GEORGE WEST en route to the
Alhambra. The Royal Illusionist CHRIS CHARLTON came to Leith in
1921 as did LINDA SINGH the Hoodoo Sorceress who presented her
fabled miracles of the Eastern world as never witnessed before on the
British stage. A mix of variety, revue, drama and plays were staged at
the Alhambra until 1930. It functioned as a cinema until March 1958 and
was demolished in 1974.

Chapter
Eight

"Falkirk Fare"

Falkirk

Falkirk

Earliest theatres in Falkirk were a portable type in the Callendar Riggs, an arrangement which changed on Christmas Day 1903 when the more permanent Grand Theatre and Opera House opened in Vicar Street. Built from plans by the Hamilton architect Alexander Cullen, it seated 2200. Opera, drama, revue and comedies brought by managing director Mr. R. C. Buchanan had limited appeal, and control passed to the B.F. Picture and Variety Circuits in 1925. Patrons were well catered for, especially those fond of a dram, with five bars available for their needs. All to no avail however and the Grand Theatre closed in 1929 prior to its reconstruction into a film house now the home of the Cannon cinema.

While the Grand with its heavier productions was failing, Falkirk's other theatre with the less grandoise name was flourishing with its repertoire of films and variety acts. Originally the Erskine Church in Silver Row, the Electric Theatre was opened in 1910 by show business promoter Teddy Atkinson after spending £2000 on renovating the main body of the church.

Initially silent films were shown, but by Christmas 1913 the Scotch character comedian DONALD MACKAY and THE BALMORALS musical vocal group were at the Electric accompanied by a resident orchestra led by OTTO ZEBLOCK. The stage was transformed in April 1921 by the new manager, a Mr. Lewis. Apart from producing and appearing in vaudeville acts throughout America and Europe, Mr. Lewis was a capable trick cyclist and roller skater. Around this time the Electric was renamed Empire.

In 1938 the interior of the theatre was gutted. Central heating and tip-up seats were installed in the auditorium and the building was rewired. A band forum was constructed allowing members of the orchestra to leave and enter their stations, without disrupting the front row of the stalls. Remaining under the management of Mr. H. Lipman but now called the "Roxy", the refurbished theatre welcomed the King of Swing, BILLY MASON and his Orchestra of thirteen players and three crooners for the re-opening in October 1938.

The world's strongest youth WILFRED BRITON pulled a bus with his teeth through the streets adjoining the Roxy as a publicity stunt. Australian escapologist MURRAY (real name Norman Murray Walters) was tied into a strait jacket and hoisted on a crane before releasing himself and discarding the constraint to the bemused spectators below — all in the cause of boosting the Roxy box office returns! Others who did this without resorting to such extreme measures were G. H. ELLIOTT; THE HOUSTON SISTERS; TOMMY MORGAN; JACK RADCLIFFE; ROBERT WILSON; GRACE CLARK & COLIN MURRAY; CHIC MURRAY & MAIDIE, and JACK LYNDON.

Stage, film and television star MAX BYGRAVES got a start at the humble Roxy in 1943 when serving with the RAF at Grangemouth. With a fellow rookie, the Bermondsey lad enacted a sketch in which he played the sergeant and his mate the raw recruit. For their eleven minutes exposure they received £11 between them!

Associated with the Empire and Roxy for nearly forty years, Falkirk's old man of showbusiness Dave Hunter staged its last show in March 1958. The Roxy was pulled down in February 1961 as the east end development scheme got under way and is now the home of the Metropolitan Hotel. Since its demise, light entertainment in Falkirk has taken the form mainly of one night engagements convened by the District Council in the Town Hall, ideal for concerts but too large for occasions that require a more hospitable setting. However, this will be rectified if proposals to convert the listed stables near Callendar House into a 300 seat Park Theatre materialize.

Chapter Nine

"Fife Funsters"

Cowdenbeath

Dunfermline

Kirkcaldy

Leven

Cowdenbeath

Once known as the "Chicago of Fife" when twenty pits worked within a three miles radius of the town, Cowdenbeath had its Empire Theatre for the first two decades of this century. Coal miners scratching a frugal living from the depths of the land and their impoverished families sought respite from the daily grind in the gay and convivial atmosphere of their local music hall.

Harry McKelvie's prestigious pantomimes transferred to Cowdenbeath from their base at the Royal Princess's Theatre Glasgow — an April event eagerly anticipated throughout Fife, especially when comedian and penny-whistle player SAM THOMSON was principal in fifty strong casts. Special late cars to Lochgelly, Kelty, Crossgates and Dunfermline were laid on at the completion of each performance for the convenience of clients who had arrived from other areas of the Kingdom. Proprietor George Penman ran cine-variety until the professional "turns" were replaced with twice weekly "Go as You Please" contests. The Empire switched to full time films in 1922.

Dunfermline

Fife's first purpose built music hall was erected in Dunfermline twixt Guildhall Street and what is now Music Hall Lane in 1852. Called after the proprietor William Clark, it comprised of three halls. Two galleries added to the main hall for exhibitions brought the seating capacity up to 2000. Below this a smaller room was used as the city's Corn Exchange while a third hall for 600, to the front of the building, was a forum for drama companies.

Dramatic plays, soirees, concerts, bazaars and dancing were all part of the scene at Clark's Music Hall where the CHRISTY MINSTRELS COMPANY were often on hand. In February 1888 a large crystal tank filled with water was wheeled in for world champion scientific swimmer PROFESSOR BEATON and daughter ANNIE to display feats of skill underwater including eating, drinking, smoking, writing and musicianship. Stirring times! Closed in January 1898 and converted into a printing press ten months later, it re-emerged in October 1913 as the La Scala Picture House. Irreverently known as the "Scratcher", it was destroyed by fire in April 1924.

The erection of St. Margaret's Hall in 1878 hastened the demise of Clark's Music Hall. With a £1300 organ, better facilities and seating for 1400, it was used extensively for music hall, drama, public meetings, festivals and fairs. DURWARD LELY in "Rob Roy" and MACKENZIE MURDOCH'S MERRY MAKERS set the resepctive melodramatic and concert patterns in the Edwardian era. Fife miner poet JOE CORRIE presented his "In Time of Strife" drama portraying the mining community's hardships during and after the 1926 General Strike. His plays toured most of Scotland's music halls appealing through their realism and poignant use of Fife dialect.

Consumed by fire in 1961, St Margaret's is best remembered by a later generation as a dance hall.

OPERA HOUSE

Few theatres attracted as much press and media attention as Dunfermline's Opera House when threatened with extinction. Acrimonious debate and correspondence with arguments and counter claims for its preservation culminated in 1982 when the Secretary of State bowed to commercial pressures and sealed its fate. Or so it seemed. The spotlight was to fall again on the Opera House, but only metaphorically.

Used as a furniture repository after ceasing operations as a theatre in 1955, listing provision ensured that its plasterwork would be saved. Decorations on the boxes, the front of the circle and gallery were painstakingly dismantled and numbered along with the proscenium and ceiling mouldings. When the thespians of Saratoga in Florida learnt of this latent treasure, they moved quickly to evaluate its potential as an element in their Performing Arts Centre. They didn't need a second invitation to acquire the remains of the Opera House which were shipped across the Atlantic in 1988 and resurrected as the heart of a mammoth theatrical complex.

Constructed from plans made by architect Roy Jackson at a cost of £6000, the Opera House accommodated 1300. The orchestra stalls, pit stalls and pit on the ground floor were skirted by the elliptical proscenium arch containing two tiers of boxes on each side of the 41ft by 28ft stage. The circle and gallery tiers were supported on iron columns and a heavy iron railing stretched across the front of the gallery . A special feature of the gas-lit theatre was the domed ceiling.

Hansel night was 11th September 1903 when local amateur dramatic clubs presided. The following week brought, appropriately, J. W. Turner's

Grand English Opera Company to Reform Street. The standard of equipment and facilities failed to meet the needs of bigger touring companies and little was seen of lyrical drama thereafter. Musical comedies were the order of most evenings when Mr. Potts was manager. After a two years closure, the Opera House got under way again on 30th December 1912 with "The Chocolate Soldier" comic opera from the Lyric Theatre in London. The theatre had been reconstructed from floor to ceiling and was now lit throughout by electricity. Sole proprietor and manager John Henry Hare, brother of comedian ROBERTSON HARE of English stage fame, added variety to seasons of repertory.

During a second closure of two years the interior was completely remodelled. The addition of a circle lounge and projection room and the replanning of the circle and rake of the gallery had the effect of reducing seating capacity to 900. These changes further enhanced the intimacy of the Opera House which had Hippodrome added to its title. A new era started in August 1921 with GEORGE WEST and KITTY EVELYN in the "Keep Guessing" revue. TOMMY LORNE; WILL FYFFE; CHARLIE KEMBLE, and NELSON JACKSON (humourist at the piano) were a few of the celebrities to make innumerable appearances in variety and revue at the Hippodrome & Opera House.

Ownership passed to a local concern under the direction of Mr. J. O'Driscoll in September 1935. Repertory with the Charles Denville Players and others met with limited support and it was Fife's premier variety theatre that the Opera House was best known thereafter. Illusionists CECIL LYLE and the GREAT LEVANTE; chorus singer FLORRIE FORDE; character actor and comedian JACK RADCLIFFE; impressionist AFRIQUE; tenor ROBERT WILSON; and comedians JIMMY LOGAN, TOMMY HOPE and JIMMY LANG are names to conjure during this period of the theatre's history.

Soon after celebrating its jubilee, manager Robert Walker was obliged to restrict twice nightly performances to Saturday with only one house during the week — a sure sign of the havoc wreaked by television on live entertainment. It came as no surprise when the heavily painted drop cloth fell for the last time on 26th March 1955 in the company of singers MASTER JOE PETERSON; GEORGE CORMACK & IRENE SHARP, and ANDY STEWART.

The final chapter had still to be enacted in the history of Dunfermline's Opera House when its greatest transformation was reserved for its Florida destination. Hollywood's BURT REYNOLDS was among the dignitaries joining the first night throng on 27th January 1990 for the recreated Opera House's dedication performance of Shaw's "Man and Superman."

Kirkcaldy

The Kings was the first permanent theatre to be contructed in Kirkcaldy, prior to which the Corn Exchange had been the main centre for travelling companies. DURWARD LELY who specialised in Scottish plays like "Guy Mannering" and "Rob Roy"; the "modern Paganini" MACKENZIE MURDOCH, who teamed up with HARRY LAUDER; and minstrel W. F. FRAME made annual visits.

With a stage of generous 60ft by 30ft proportions, the spacious playhouse first known as the Kings opened on 14th November 1904. Erected at a cost of £20,000 to plans prepared by local architect J. D. Swanson it seated 2000 with standing room for 500. Lighting was by gas chandeliers, and to provide adequate ventilation the roof was designed to slide back so that the audience could literally see the stars from the stalls. The policy of booking drama and musical comedies was misguided and when this venture failed the Kings was snatched up by the Bostock conglomerate at a knocked down price of £7000. Renamed the Hippodrome, it re-opened on 16th March 1908 with IVAN TSCHERNOFF'S group of ponies and dogs, and the champion long boot (42ins) dancer of the world. The emphasis switched from plays to music hall, a policy which was maintained after 1916 when it became the Opera House.

The stage and auditorium were rebuilt in 1937 when it became the Regal cinema, the precursor of today's A.B.C. in the same building which embarked as the Kings Theatre some 86 years ago in the "Auld Toun's" High Street.

Leven

With the exception of the Second World War years when it was requisitioned by the Army, the Beach Pavilion was a fertile forum for summer concert parties from 1929 until 1965. Placing Leven in the forefront as a seaside and pleasure resort over the years were comedian IAN MACLEAN; singer BALLARD BROWN, and promoter Arthur

Abbie. The post war years saw the lanky TOMMY HOOD elevating galusness into a fine art form in a succession of summer revues in which GLEN DALY was also much to the fore.

Doubling as a cinema and dance hall, the Jubilee Theatre (formerly the Town Hall) staged occasional July and August revues. The 1936 bumper bill saw JACK RADCLIFFE and HELEN NORMAN in charge of comedy; vocalists TOM F. MOSS; SUTTON & DONELLI and THE FOUR SMITH BROTHERS; accordionists McKENZIE REID & DOROTHY; THE GERRARD SISTERS and a troupe of EIGHT CHARLTON GIRLS. ALEX MUNRO breezed into Leven to lead the 1951 revue after which the Jubilee reverted to its more familiar guise as a dance hall before giving way to road developments in 1973.

And so the once lively Leven was left bereft of any theatrical activity as live entertainment in beach pavilions took second place to the wonders of modern media science.

Chapter
Ten

"Stirling Smiles"

Stirling

Stirling

Shut down as a fire risk in 1939, evidence of the old Alhambra still remains in the form of the pay box and stairs leading to the circle, gallery and side balconies. The original stage and dressing rooms are now used as furniture showrooms within the Arcade shopping centre.

With seating for 1200, the Alhambra ran films for the greater part of the week with variety restricted to two houses on Saturday. Exceptions to this routine were made when the bigger names came to Stirling. Among these were character comedienne and dancer MISS FRANCES LETTY assisted by her ragtime pianist; Royal magician CHRIS CHARLTON; revelations in wooden shoe dancing from coon JIM E. SULLIVAN; the FIVE WHITELEYS in their wire walking acrobatic musical melange, cigarette king DAVALAN in mystery and mirth; AL BERTINO and his Music Swingers; and the Irish American play-boy SAM RAYNE.

The Alhambra always made a strong appeal to festive season pleasure seekers, and pantomimes and road shows in which TOMMY MORGAN, CHARLIE KEMBLE and BOBBY TELFORD were accompanied by Jimmy Running and his pit orchestra are readily recalled by an older generation.

Chapter
Eleven

"Northern Lights"

Aberdeen

Aberdeen

ALHAMBRA

Aberdeen's Tarnty Kirk on the corner of Guild Street and Exchange Street was converted into the Alhambra music hall with William McFarland the first proprietor before he moved along to Her Majesty's in September 1881. The Livermore Brothers then operated it as a less expensive companion hall to the Palace Theatre. Business was transferred temporarily to the cramped and inadequate quarters of the Alhambra while the Palace was rebuilt after the 1896 fire.

The adjoining cobbled streets were a hive of activity with pedestrians and horse-drawn traffic. Slum properties and unprepossessing drinking dives were in close proximity to the harbour, making the Alhambra an ideal platform for vaudevillians who could offer a brief respite from the daily slog that was the lot for Victorian working folk.

Latterly, it housed a waxworks and menagerie as well as presenting music hall and cinematograph. Also known as the Winter Zoo, it assumed its original name of Alhambra when the animals returned to their summer base at the beach. The end came in May 1910, two months ahead of the re-opening of the city's best known theatre — the Tivoli.

BEACH PAVILION

The old Pavilion of wooden walls and corrugated roof was replaced in May 1928 with a more solid construction as part of an ambitious development scheme on the Esplanade. Built with indifferent heating arrangements which took little account of the vagaries of the climate and furnished for £9500, it seated 750 on one floor.

To reflect on this building is to recall the summer months between the wars when Harry Gordon was resident tenant. The greatest indigenous exponent of the North East sense of humour, HARRY GORDON first gained prominence in pierrot shows and concert parties in Stonehaven and Aberdeen. He had an innate gift for portaying Buchan characterisations, wifies (more oftan than not without their teeth), and functionaries of the mythical Inversnecky village community. Clean, canny, couthie humour and sketches with JACK HOLDEN as the ideal aide and aptly billed as "In with the fittings" were the basic ingredients of the concert parties hosted by the "Laird O'Inversnecky".

Accompanied by pianist ALICE STEPHENSON working her fingers

to the bone, a number of big names of stage and concert hall guested with Harry Gordon's Entertainers. Thus it was that a young GERTRUDE LAWRENCE; actor JACK WARNER; musical comedy star JOSE COLLINS; whispering baritone JACK SMITH; Viennese singers ANNE ZEIGLER & WEBSTER BOOTH; the upper crust raconteur duo of WESTERN BROTHERS, and violinist DE GROOT made their way to the Pavilion on the sea-front. Glamour was provided by the dancing troupe of FOUR TILLER GIRLS — an innovation in seaside summer shows in the thirties. Not prepared to lower standards, and finding that spells of unseasonable weather made Aberdeen's beach an uninviting spot for an evening's entertainment, Harry gave up the tenancy in 1940. The Pavilion never recovered from his departure to team up with WILL FYFFE, ALEC FINLAY; JIMMY LOGAN and other Scots celebrities in pantomime and revue.

Dormant throughout the war, there was a flurry of activity in the early 1950s when the three harmonising BEVERLEY SISTERS; pianist KAY CAVENDISH, and comedian DICK EMERY guested in shows compered by MORECOMBE & WISE. Local artistes whose careers started at the Beach Pavilion included CHARLES STEWART of the Fol-de-Rols and singing sisters ANNE & LAURA BRAND. Closed in 1961, it became the Gaiety licensed restaurant two years later and now regales as the Mediterranean-style Cafe Continental.

But let the "Laird 'Imsel" have the last word. As he was wont to remind us in fable and song, his Pavilion audiences comprised of:—
"City fouk, country fouk, Torry fouk
Fittie fouk, fouk fae Constitution Street
and fouk fae Rubislaw Den and
far beyond".

PALACE THEATRE

The original construction with a fifty foot frontage to Bridge Place and rear to Crown Terrace was built as a circus for John Henry Cooke in 1888. Acquired by title-conscious proprietors Baron Zeigler and Major Widdman in November 1891, they replaced the wooden structure and canvas top with granite walls and a timber roof in their Jollity Royal Vaudeville Theatre before selling out to the Livermore Brothers in 1893.

Disaster struck the People's Palace on the night of 30th September, 1896. Just after the second act had been completed by eccentric comedians and dancers O'CONNER & MARTREY a red glare was seen through the drop scene. Fire had broken out when the top of the flies came into contact with one of the gas lights, and in next to no time flames rapidly shot between the curtains and through the roof before seizing on the wooden interior and framework. The fleeing audience were hampered in the wild rush for the exits by the narrow passages and steep tiers in the galleries. Seven people perished in the fiery furnace with many others scarred by flame and falling timbers.

Costing £15,000 to build in the Italian Venetian style of architecture, the Palace re-opened on 28th October, 1898 with 1800 seats and standing room for 1400. There were ten rows of orchestra stalls with pit stalls below the side galleries and the grand circle running round three sides of the building. The promenade at the back of the balcony could accommodate 300 with over 500 cramped into wooden forms in the amphitheatre and upper gallery.

The spacious 38ft wide by 34ft deep stage was crossed by CHARLIE CHAPLIN on three weekly engagements. First with "Casey's Court" as a Dead-end Kid, then with eight Lancashire Lads as a dancer, and latterly in Fred Karno's "Mumming Birds" sketch before leaving these shores for Hollywood in 1910. Imprisoned in a strait jacket and sack and dumped in the Albert Quay dock, escapologist HARRY HOUDINI surfaced to perform heroics in a padded cell and zinc lined piano case on a Palace stage adorned with a 120 guineas tableau curtain.

Scotch comedians to please Bon Accord audiences were W. F. FRAME; HARRY LAUDER; WILL FYFFE, and Aberdonian JACK LORIMER, father of comedy dancer and actor MAX WALL. Another son of the North-East who pulled the crowds to Bridge Place was miracle worker DR. WALFORD BODIE. Actor vocalist GEORGE LASHWOOD bade "Goodbye Dolly Gray"; graceful soft shoe dancer EUGENE STRATTON gave "Lily of Laguna"; TOM COSTELLO sang "Comrades"; coster comedian GUS ELEN pushed his "barrer"; CHARLES COBURN "broke the bank at Monte Carlo"; gormless JACK PLEASANTS rendered his own creation "Twenty one today"; LITTLE TICH danced in out-size boots; and ju jitsu king YOKIO TANI weaved paths around baffled wrestlers.

Improvements to the auditorium preceded a buy out by the Tivoli landlords in 1911. Pictures were introduced for part of the programme before a new figure arrived on Aberdeen's theatrical horizon in August 1925 in the person of ARTHUR HINTON. Old fashioned melodrama in which virtuous heroines (often played by his wife PEGGY COURTNEY) triumphed over bold bad villains were staged by Hinton's stock company for three years.

Sold for £16,000 to Jack Poole in February 1929, the Palace was reconditioned as a cinema — a function it fulfilled for nearly thirty years. It was then launched as Aberdeen's largest ballroom with one large balcony by Top Rank in March 1960. Live bands were dispensed with in keeping with modern trends, in 1976. As Ritzy's the old People's Palace, the upper parts of which remain more or less intact above a false ceiling, was voted Scotland's Number One Discotheque in 1988/89.

TIVOLI THEATRE

City fathers and lesser mortals were out in numbers for the inauguration of Her Majesty's Opera House on 19th December, 1872. And a spectacular sight they beheld! The three storey Venetian Gothic looking building with its coloured and banded voussoir stones to the arches provided an imposing facade of bold design. Concrete was used for the first time on any significant scale in Scotland for the side and back walls. It was a fitting tribute to the first specialist theatre architect Charles Phipps and his local adviser on the project, James Matthews, a future Lord Provost of Aberdeen. His best efforts, however, were reserved for the interior. Lit from the ceiling by sunlight in a 35ft diameter cornice, the gracefully curved auditorium accommodated 1744. The six boxes sat 44; fauteuils 120; pit stalls and promenade 480; circle 400; while 700 squatted on benches in the gods. The cost of this unique Victorian gem was £8400.

As a home of drama, Her Majesty's (the more grandoise part of the title was dropped in 1881) maintained an active theatrical presence for the next 34 years. It proved a worthy showcase for legit greats OSMOND TEARLE; BEERBOHM TREE; EDWARD COMPTON; ELLEN TERRY and SIR HENRY IRVING at the turn of the century.

The doyen of theatre architects, Frank Matcham, improved safety precautions and venitalation before carrying out a major scheme of internal reconstruction at a cost of £10,000 in 1909. There is little doubt that the auditorium owes its present intimate proportions, opulent Baroque-style plasterwork and circular ceiling with its framed painted panels to this work. Another Matcham masterpiece had taken over the role of Aberdeen's straight theatre in December 1906 when the Robert Arthur Company transferred their allegiance and pocket books to the new His Majesty's in Schoolhill. The older established theatre in Guild Street re-opened on 18th July, 1910 as the Tivoli with music hall and revue the staple fare.

MISS MARIE KENDAL — 1917

XVII

WILL FYFFE — 1926

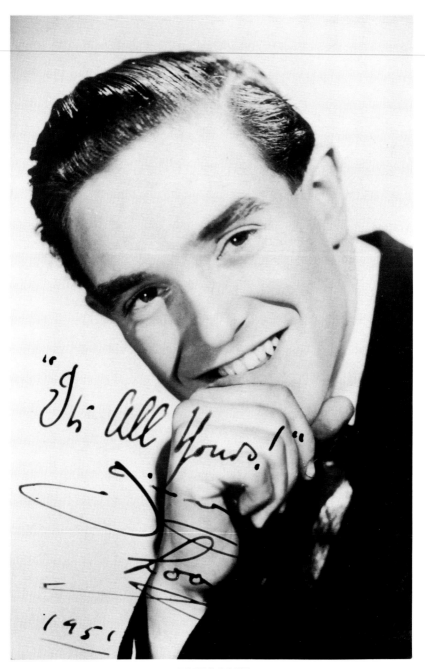

"It's All Yours!"
Jimmy Logan
1951

JIMMY LOGAN

XIX

SINGING STARS OF MUSICAL COMEDY — GWEN OVERTON & CLIVE STOCK

DANCERS OF DISTINCTION — IRENE CAMPBELL & DANNY REGAN

XXI

ANDY STEWART

BEACH PAVILION LEVEN, SUMMER SEASON 1947

TOMMY HOOD & SUMMERS CONCERT PARTY — LEVEN, early 1950's

Twice nightly houses started with an overture by the grand orchestra of ten instrumentalists led by JACK SHEPHERD. This was a prelude for eight turns, who had to please by virtue of their specialist talents and unmicrophoned voices with a backcloth as their only visible means of support. Among their numbers was the bulbous-nosed eccentric W. C. FIELDS who appeared on the Tivoli's fourth programme as a comedy juggler in his pre-Hollywood days — a scene far removed from the world-wide film audiences he would later enthral.

Other early arrivals were "Strathspey King" JAMES SCOTT SKINNER who blazed the trail for today's traditional fiddlers. Another virtuoso of the violin and composer, HAYDN WOOD, made four bill-topping appearances accompanied by pianist DOROTHY COURT. He achieved lasting fame for his composition of "Roses of Picardy". Entertainment of the drawing room order was provided by pianists MARGARET COOPER and HARRY FRAGSON; Royal pianist ELSIE SOUTHGATE, and actor mimic BRANSBY WILLIAMS in his repertoire of Dickens' characters. Scotland's greatest character actor and comedian WILL FYFFE made his first of eleven Tivoli engagements in December 1917. An immediate success, his appeal never waned for three decades during which he reached the top of his profession on stage and screen. With his uncanny command of the country's dialect, WILL FYFE held a unique place in Scottish affections.

The lanky master of mannerisms and unrelated nonsense TOMMY LORNE, brought out the laughs with his mournful and unpredictable facial expressions. "Scotland's Charlie Chaplin", DAVE WILLIS, the wee man with the twinkling eyes and feet projected a style of daftness and clowning that had the stamp of comic genius. Both were firm favourites in Tivoli revues. Held in similar esteem with twelve bill-topping weekly programmes to her credit throughout the twenties and thirties was FLORRIE FORDE. Whether in music hall or as pantomime's principal boy she won universal acclaim for her chorus songs with the lusty lyrics. It was a sad day in the annals of the Tivoli's history when she died on 18th April, 1940 returning to the theatre after entertaining wounded sailors at Kingseat. An acknowledged home for the big names in music hall, the Tivoli welcomed Cockney character comedienne LILY MORRIS, dandy raconteur ALBERT WHELAN; quick change burlesque comedian G. S. MELVIN; light comedian RANDOLPH SUTTON: male impersonator HETTY KING; soft shoe dancer and singer G. H. ELLIOTT and a host of artistes of lesser fame.

The names of magicians and illusionists DAVID DEVANT; RAMESES; CARMO; CECIL LYLE; CHUNG LING SOO; HORACE GOLDIN and DANTE loomed large on Tivoli posters. Big bands which forsook their exclusive hotel bases in London for stays at the North-East citadel of variety included DEBROY SOMERS; ROY FOX; SYDNEY LIPTON: TROISE and his MANDOLIERS; FELIX MENDELSSOHN's HAWAIIAN SERENADERS and PRIMO SCALA and his ACCORDIONISTS.

A change of ownership in 1938 saw Horace Collins continuing in his role as managing director. This coincided with a comprehensive facelift which returned the theatre to its former livery. The reduced 1049 capacity comprised five rows of fauteuils for 108, behind which the nine rows of pits stalls sat 236. Three rows of 92 seats in the Grand Circle, six rows of 187 in the Upper Circle, ten cushioned benches in the Gallery for 387 and four handsome boxes completed the picture in the gloriously extravagant auditorium made brighter by the decorator and new lighting effects.

Paradoxically, theatres enjoyed a purple patch during and after the Hitler war. Long queues extending to Carmelite Lane and Stirling Street ahead of the second house curtain rising were a familiar sight. Not surprising in view of the quality of output and standing of the celebrities arriving at the cheery house of variety in Guild Street. Names that come readily to mind are pianists RAWICZ & LANDAUER; TURNER LAYTON and CHARLIE KUNZ, stage and screen comedian FRED EMNEY; quick change actor OWEN McGIVENEY; ventriloquist ARTHUR PRINCE; and singers ELIZABETH WELCH and MONTE REY.

Part of this wide world of diverse entertainment was the musical duo of TED ANDREWS & BARBARA. On their third Tivoli date in 1945 they introduced daughter JULIE, a slip of a lass who sang like an exultation of larks. She was none other than JULIE ANDREWS, destined to become a Broadway star of musicals "Mary Poppins" and "The Sound of Music."

The style and shape of shows changed after the war when weekly engagements became the exception and road shows were taken out by leading Scottish comedians and/or singers. The whimsical and debonair JACK ANTHONY first arrived at the Tivoli as an anonymous light comedian in 1936. Thereafter he came to the theatres which gave him a break for fifteen successive years in "Giggles and Girls" revues. The dapper cheerful figure of ALEC FINLAY in National attire was a familiar sight for the best part of thirty years in "Finlay Frolics". He readily adapted to television where his wide ranging talents from bagpipe playing, dancing and narrating comic songs won him the award of Grampian's Personality of 1972. JACK RADCLIFFE'S "Revels" gave scope for the natural character comedian to express his acting skills in a blend of comedy and pathos with leading lady HELEN NORMAN.

The carefree spirit of music hall in a comfortable unpretentous setting was seldom better manifested than in the Tivoli's long running "Whirl of Laughter" summer shows of the fifties. Much of the credit for their appeal goes to comedian JACK MILROY with his captivating personality and infectious humour. No theatre was bound up with the lives and careers of JACK MILROY and his wife MARY LEE more than Aberdeen's Tivoli, for it was here that she made her initial stage entrance as a singing starlet with ROY FOX'S BAND and it was while headlining at the same theatre in 1952 that they married. The following year genial JACK MILROY set the record for the Tivoli's longest running show of 22 weeks — a total of 264 consecutive performances!

The name of ROBERT WILSON was legion in Scottish theatrical circles, and nowhere more than at Aberdeen's Tivoli did the "Voice of Scotland" enjoy a faithful following who came frae a' airts individually, in families, wedding groups and bus parties to wonder at his impeccable tone, diction and breath control. Combining a generous personality and stage presence with exquisite singing of Scottish ballads and airs, his appeal was reflected in broken box office returns by his WHITE HEATHER GROUP. Helping to exhale the spirit of Caledonia in these all tartan productions were Britain's best button key accordionist WILL STARR; tenor GORDON MACKENZIE; musical clown BILLY CROTCHET; and Country and Western aspirant destined to hit the big time, SYDNEY DEVINE. No one was better equipped to take over the mantle of ROBERT WILSON than versatile ANDY STEWART who had won universal recognition and a silver disc with his record of a "Scottish Soldier."

Ownership of the Tivoli passed to the Wm. Galt theatrical syndicate in January 1954. An invaluable addition to the Dundee Palace, Edinburgh Palladium, Paisley Victory and Leith Gaiety music halls already under their jurisdiction, the Tivoli was the brightest jewel in their crown and remains, to this day the only theatre in that circuit to have avoided the ravages of commercial developers. The orchestra which had been conducted by CLIFFORD JORDAN for twelve years was reduced in numbers to five with JOHNNY DOUGLAS directing from the piano. ANDREW

FOLEY became manager — an office he handled with quiet efficiency and tact to the benefit of patrons and performers alike for nine years.

Resident revues continued to account for the greater part of the Tivoli output with stalwarts of the Galt circuit figuring regularly in twice nightly sessions of spirited fun, song and dance. Foremost in this group were JOHNNY VICTORY with his spicy mix of earthy humour and monologues and LEX McLEAN comfirming his status as Scotland's pre-eminent comedian with unrivalled timing, witty improprieties and a fund of hilarious sketches. The rich tradition of the North-East character and indigenous comedy was maintained by ROLAND SMITH and gifted exponent of the Doric ROBBIE SHEPHERD while local soprano EVELYN HENRY and accordionists AILEEN MANSON and ALICE DAVIDSON made significant contributions.

The Tivoli owed a special debt to Gaelic singer CALUM KENNEDY. As well as leading revues in tartan display, he adapted to the role of impressario when the potent counter attractions of television and bingo had forced the closure of variety theatres the length and breadth of the land. Instrumental in bringing headliners MOIRA ANDERSON, with her classical singing voice; stage and screen star ANNE SHELTON; debonair crooner FRANKIE VAUGHAN; ebullient showman BILLY COTTON; song and dance man extraordinaire DICKIE HENDERSON; and the complex comic clown TONY HANCOCK to the Tivoli footlights, Calum's sterling efforts culminated on 2nd April, 1966 with the final drop of the drapes.

An Arts Council report of 1978 extolled the virtues of the Tivoli as a potential home for a full-sized repertory company. Their findings stressed the need to ensure that this magnificent example of an intimate theatre boasting the work of both the country's foremost architects was maintained in a favourable condition for the eventual restoration of live theatre within its walls. Aberdeen has in His Majesty's Theatre an impressive and large touring house but has no home for a resident drama company. The Tivoli with its 29ft by 27ft stage, seating capacity for 800, gloriously extravagant auditorium, and greater degree of intimacy would fit such a role ideally.

Afforded the protection of statutory listing, the Tivoli has suffered no major alterations since the introduction of bingo. Even the box which housed the stage spot lighting or "limes" and from which single slide advertisements were projected at the interval has been retained. Sensitively restored to its original splendour by proprietors Top Flight Leisure Ltd., and poised to offer occasional music hall and cabaret, it is hoped that the cry of "full house" at Aberdeen's oldest theatre will soon revert to its original meaning.

Chapter
Twelve

"Lanarkshire Laughs"

Airdrie
Hamilton
Motherwell

Airdrie

The only tangible evidence which remains of a once flourishing music hall in the Monklands is the Rialto Bingo and Amusement Arcade in Hallcraig Street. Originally a public and fruit market, this focal point housed shooting galleries, boxing booths and the side shows associated with a fairground until it was transformed into the Hippodrome in 1908 by James Loudon. A reconstruction in 1911 dispensed with the old shop fronts and a sloping floor was installed in the hall.

Best remembered by past generations of Airdrieonians were kilted tenor J. M. HAMILTON brandishing a broad sword and taking the Hippodrome by storm with his rendering of "McGregor's Gathering"; soprano NELLIE McNAB, and violinist and composer of the Scottish ballad "Hame o' Mine" MACKENZIE MURDOCH. From further afield comedienne LILLIE LANGTRY; FLO DIXIE the bantam male impersonator; mystery man MORRITT; quick change artiste CORA CORINA; Indian musical genius DOROSWAMI; and the Latvian Hercules MARTIN BREEDIS who issued a £50 challenge to anyone emulating his feats of strength, all made the journey to the Hippodrome.

The highlight of many weeks was the Friday night amateur competitions when local beauties, singers, ballroom dancers, melodeon players, and clog dancers vied for cash prizes. Billed as "Airdrie's Own Komik", JACK RADCLIFFE appeared weeks before the Hippodrome closed for redecoration and the installation of central heating in June 1929. One of the Scotland's best character comedians and actors he depicted the drunk with uncanny accuracy on stages throughout the U.K., Australia and the States. Re-opened on 30th September 1929, as the Rialto with cine variety it went over to full-time "flicks" nine years later. This gave way to bingo in 1962 and now embraces the Big Apple discotheque, amusement arcade and bingo complex.

In neighbouring Coatbridge the old music hall style of single turns had a thirty years run at the Empire before public taste changed in favour of films. The Theatre Royal publicised "fun, frolic, fast and furious" for fifty years with such luminaries as comedians JOCK MILLS and HARRY KORRIS; and magicians DAVID DEVANT and DR. ROYAL RACEFORD. Its ever changing repertoire of variety, revues, plays and pictures lasted until road developments took its final toll.

Hamilton

The earliest permanent home for the presentation of concerts, melodrama and variety was the Victoria Halls in Quarry Street. Designed by local architect Andrew Downie, this substantial three storey edifice of red free stone cost £4000. Comfort was not a primary consideration for the capacity 1500 who were sat on forms with back rails and iron supports in the pit and side galleries and in opera chairs with perforated bottoms at the front of the gallery. Within three years of opening in 1887 the lesser Victoria Halls had catered for HARRY LAUDER'S wedding reception four years ahead of his call in a professional capacity. His mentor, W. F. FRAME, made many appearances in Hamilton as "the Man U Know" and the "Apostle of Fun" until his death in 1919.

Renamed the Playhouse, the theatre was bought by the proprietor of the neighbouring Hippodrome, Mr. E. H. Bostock, in 1908. Having made the interior more comfortable and attractive, he inauguruated bioscopic pictures with the emphasis on educative productions. It was not until 1st December 1947 that the Playhouse, latterly called the Granada Cinema, reverted to live shows when it re-opened as the Granada Variety Theatre with JIMMY BENSON and JACK CARR principal funsters.

For the next ten years, two houses on Friday and Saturday was the standard format in which DAVE WILLIS; TOMMY HOOD; BILLY RUSK; ANDY STEWART; crooner LARRY DAVIS and Scotland's "Norman Wisdom" JIMMY WARREN were hits before the Granada expired in April 1958. The former Victoria Halls was to suffer the ultimate indignity — conversion of the ground floor to a television showroom promoting the medium which had hastened its end as a forum for live entertainment.

HIPPODROME

Built mainly of wood and metal for the Bostock circus and menagerie family, it seemed inevitable that the Hippodrome would ultimately succumb to fire. Those worst fears were realised on Burns' Night 1946 when the corner of Townhead Street was a smouldering mass of corrugated iron sheeting, blackened timber and metal and the Hippodrome was no more.

It was a far cry from the opening night on 14th October 1907 when the proud proprietor declared "We insist on the same healthy tone throughout the performances and impress upon the artistes that no element in the audience must tempt them to swerve from that refinement which on the part of Mr. & Mrs. Bostock and those by whom they are surrounded is innate''. These exacting standards were observed by cockney character comedienne LILY MORRIS of "the Old Apple Tree", and "Why am I always the Bridesmaid?" fame; comic singer GEORGE FORMBY, Senior; the crazy band of TEN LOONIES and FRED KARNO'S gangs in the early days of the Hippodrome. DR. BODIE mesmerised audiences with his hypnotism, illusions and electric wizardry, while comedians HARRY GORDON; GEORGE WEST; DAVE WILLIS, and TOMMY MORGAN set the pace between the wars.

Motherwell

Best remembered by an older generaion for its melodrama, the New Century Theatre in Windmill Street purveyed live theatre from 1902 until 1934. One of the most handsome temples of entertainment in Scotland, it brought temporary light relief to industrial workers and their families who had survived short and no working weeks of the Depression years.

The advent of 1911 saw a new venture known as the Electric Theatre display cinematograph pictures on the screen followed by five variety turns. Situated at the corner of Camp Street and Parkhead Street the building was bought, by Walter Thompson at Christmas 1916. The policy of supplying the latest pictures of notable events and variety turns was maintained throughout the twenties. It was appropriate that the electrifying wizard DR. WALFORD BODIE was the biggest crowd puller to the Electric Empire.

Touring variety companies were unable to command sizeable audiences most nights for their week's hiring of the hall and by 1937 performances were restricted to two nights per week on Friday and Saturday with six day sessions restricted to the festive season. Principal comedy producers around this time were HARRY GORDON; TOMMY LOMAN; CHARLIE KEMBLE; JOHNNY RAE, and JIMMY BENSON.

During the war years and the fifties when the Empire was manged by Arthur Simmons; JACK MAYO; BERT BENDON; JIMMY NICOL; DIXON & HUNTER and WOOD & FRAYNE kept the fun going. Others to take the eye were NEVILLE TAYLOR (Glasgow's Own Ink Spot); polished pianist NICKY KIDD from Jack Hylton's Band and local man with strong Canadian connections JIMMY REID. Picking up the strings again after demobilisation, SONNIE ALLAN & HECTOR NICOL were billed at Motherwell's Empire as the modern musicals with voice and guitar. HECTOR NICOL was to emerge as a foil for Scotland's major comics before dominating the club scene in the seventies and early eighties as the indisputable king of clubland comedy.

The shell of the original Empire remains neglected and unoccupied within yards of the modern Civic Centre.

Chapter
Thirteen

"City of Discovery"

Dundee

Arbroath

Dundee

With the man in the street expressing little interest in the arts and culture, more humble places of entertainment known as Penny Gaffs sprang up to compete with the legitimate theatre in the 1860's. Fizzy Gow's Gaff in Lindsay Street rejoiced in the posh title of Clarence Theatre, while the Seagate Gaff was frequented by local poet McGonigal who declaimed his verses to a boisterous and unappreciative public.

The name of William McFarland is inexorably linked with the origin and progress of the music hall in Dundee. As a far sighted youth in 1870, he converted a ramshackle wooden structure forsaken by Sanger's Circus beside the East Railway Station into the Alhambra Music Hall. Decreed unsafe by the authorities, they then invited him to take over the more substantial and better equipped music hall at the foot of Castle Street. Now occupied as a printing press, tangible evidence of its music hall days exists on interior doors with etched panes of glass depicting violins and harps. McFarland was the automatic choice to manage the beleaguered Theatre Royal whose 1200 capacity was seldom taxed.

At a time when the stock company system was on its last legs and theatrical property a doubtful proposition, McFarland's next veture was the contruction of the 1700 seater Her Majesty's Theatre which was launched by public subscription to the tune of £12,000, in 1885. Sold to the Robert Arthur Company of London in 1891, its days as a straight theatre ended in December 1930 when moving people made way for moving pictures in the Majestic Cinema. Parts of the substantial walls which survived the August 1941 fire were used in the construction of the Seagate's super cinema — now the Cannon Film Centre.

PALACE THEATRE

Operated as a permanent circus for twenty years until 1891, the Livermore Brothers opened the People's Palace Music Hall on 2nd January 1893. Prior to that it had occupied a site in Lochee Road near Dudhope Crescent Road for two years during which variety was established in Dundee.

The obsolete circus ring was enclosed under the stalls and the basic interior creations lasted for the rest of the theatre's life. Run in association with the Palace Theatres in Aberdeen, Sunderland, Weymouth and Bristol, the London "swells" like GEORGE LASHWOOD and GEORGE BEAUCHAMP were early visitors. MARIE LLOYD and LITTLE TICH paved the way for a young HARRY LAUDER who hadn't his sorrows to seek at the People's Palace. Despite the proprietors claim to be "pioneers in refinement and that the Palace was the only place where you could with safety take your wives and families", Monday first houses were notoriously tough for less experienced performers. HARRY LAUDER was reputed to have been booed — a fate less cruel than that which befell a contemporary singer. "Awa' for a can!" greeted his efforts. It was as directive bellowed at apprentices in the mills when tea was required and they were expected to make themselves scarce. He appealed to the restive elements reminding them that it was his bread and butter, the same as work in the factories was theirs. They heard him out but at the second house, when he thought all would be well, a voice roared from the gallery "Here's your bread and butter". A loaf skimmed his ear as he stood a forlorn figure on the stage. Tough times at the turn of the century!

The Palace flirted with films in 1912 and became one of the 24 cinemas in movie-mad Dundee. The screen was discarded in 1938 and the Palace reverted to its true role as a house of variety. Ownership passed to the Horace Collins syndicate whose interests included the Aberdeen Tivoli; Edinburgh Theatre Royal and Liverpool Shakespeare Theatres. The best of international and home-spun acts toured this circuit with new faces and bills changing every week.

Admission prices in the forties read:—

> Orchestra stalls 3/- (15p)
> Stalls and side stalls 2/- (10p)
> Back stalls 1/6 (7p)
> Dress circle 2/- (10p)
> Family circle 1/6 (7p)
> Back and side circles 1/- (5p)

Many families found escape from the mundane working routine in the magic world that a brightly lit and cosy variety hall offered. The Palace provided that reprieve. When the Wm. Galt theatrical concern had control in the fifties, resident shows were the favoured format. JACK ANTHONY; ALEC FINLAY; ROBERT WILSON; HARRY GORDON, and JOHNNY VICTORY, all had their supporters — none more so than the latter. With his bullfrog voice, topical monologues and sketches, JOHNNY VICTORY (with help from HECTOR NICOL, BETTY NOLAN, RON COBURN and local tenor DENNIS CLANCY) was good box office.

After a brief foray into bingo in 1962, Grampian Theatres took over

ABERDEEN TIVOLI

ROBERT WILSON

XXVI

JACK MILROY

GEORGE CORMACK AND IRENE SHARP

"SCOTLAND'S SWEETHEARTS OF SONG"

GLEN DALY

JOHNNY VICTORY — 1955

The Empire Theatre

FOR ONE WEEK
Commencing MONDAY, August 19

The World-Famous Comedian:

HARRY LAUDER

As ever, new—
This time newer than ever

The REGO TWINS	THE RHYTHM KINGS
Comedy at its Highest	Modern Entertainers
DORIS ASHTON	**FRANK BOSTON**
The Paramount Star Vocalist	Royal Command Performance Juggler

BILLIE and MATT
THE FAMOUS PIANO ACCORDIONISTS

PRICES OF ADMISSION (including Tax):
Front Stalls, 3s 6d; Mid Stalls, 2s 6d; Front Balcony, 3s 6d; Balcony, 2s 6d; Back Balcony, 1s; Back Stalls, 1s 6d.

NIGHTLY at 8; Doors Open 7.30 p.m.   SATURDAY at 6.30 p.m. and 9 p.m.; Doors Open 6 p.m. and 8.30 p.m.

MATINEES :—Wednesday and Saturday at 3 p.m.; Doors Open 2.30

BOOKING OFFICE OPEN 11 to 1 and 3 to 5.

Chronicle, Inverness.

1935 PLAYBILL

XXXI

SIX BRAW LADS — Left to right: Arthur Spink, Dennis Clancy, Rob Coburn, Joss Esplin, Alec Finlay, Will Starr

in 1965 changing the name to Theatre Royal. Sell out seasons with CALUM KENNEDY, who had been the moving force behind the regeneration of the theatre, and the tartan twosome of ALEXANDER BROTHERS were recaptured when RIKKI FULTON & JACK MILROY swaggered on as "Francie & Josie". Singers FRANKIE VAUGHAN, LENA MARTELL and MOIRA ANDERSON also succeeded in filling the 1172 seat auditorium before fire destroyed the Old People's Palace on 12th October 1977. No milling crowds would again throng the Nethergate in anticipation of two hours of variety in Dundee's best remembered music hall.

KINGS THEATRE

The Kings and Hippodrome opened as a variety theatre in the Cowgate on 15th March 1909, with character actor and mimic BRANSBY WILLIAMS the main attraction. Schoolmaster comedy actor of stage and screen WILL HAY; local delineator of Scottish life and character par excellence WILL FYFFE; stilt walker ARCHIE LEACH who became known to world-wide audiences as film star CARY GRANT; the prime minister of Mirth, GEORGE ROBEY with arched eyebrows, flat bowler and seedy frock coat; and fellow knight of the music hall HARRY LAUDER were a few of the notabilities who strutted its stage. Musical plays from Daly's Theatre in London, opera, ballet and ice spectaculars on a full skating surface were testimony to the adaptibility and resources of the Kings.

The distinction of being the main theatre in the City of Discovery lasted for the Kings and Hippodrome until September 1928 when the all-pervading silver screen was installed. Renamed the Gaumont after a take over in 1956, the theatre enjoyed a renaissance hosting live performing arts and international touring companies. In its dual role as a cinema and theatre, it knew teenage idols CLIFF RICHARD; MARK WYNTER; GEORGIE FAME, balladeers JOHN HANSEN and DAVID WHIT-FIELD; and the Fol-de-Rols revue with DENNY WILLIS. This happy state of affairs continued until 1961 when the Gaumont was transformed into a super cinema. The movies only Gaumont was renamed Odeon by Rank in 1973 with bingo the staple diet.

VICTORIA

The Gaiety Theatre of Varieties functioned for seven years from 13th April 1903 in association with the Empire, Greenock and Queens and Tivoli theatres in Glasgow — a most influential combine in the days when music hall had an unparalleled hold on working folk. Manager James Creighton had a bias for strong drama and the unpredictable and so magicians and illusionists were often to the fore at the Victoria Road house, none more so than electric wizard DR. WALFORD BODIE with his galvanic assistant LA BELLE ELECTRA.

Restructured and renamed the Victoria in 1910, it welcomed comedians DAVE WILLIS; BERT MURRAY; LESTER & WOOD; WULLIE LINDSAY & JACK HOLDEN; and the exceptional FIVE SHERRY BROTHERS team of violinists, dancers and vocalists. Twice nightly variety was interspersed with films until 1935, when the Victoria went over to pictures exclusively — an arrangement which prevails to this day. The stage was incorporated within a much altered auditorium and the only unspoilt feature of the original building is the pink painted stone facade.

ALHAMBRA THEATRE

With high hopes that it would be a stronghold of variety, Arthur Henderson opened his 1050 seat Alhambra on 12th August 1929. But it wasn't to be! The dressing rooms hewn out of rock under the 58ft wide and 28ft deep stage were occupied infrequently by performers. Both cine variety and drama failed before the Bellfield Street amusement centre became the State cinema. Acquired by the council in 1975, it stages local amateur musicals and dramatics as well as professional pantomimes and variety shows in its role as the Whitehall Theatre.

Arbroath

Known as the new Public Halls from its start in 1867, this venue for touring plays and vaudeville was never a commercial proposition. It was rescued from oblivion in 1918 when the Webster family of flax manufacturers gifted the building to the Town in memory of their son killed in the fields of Flanders. From 1933, ten weeks summer seasons with the Arbroath Follies were annual events. Prior to this MELVIN'S MERRY MASCOTS and the SOURIS concert party had made do with a canvas covered fit-up stage and enclosure on the sands.

A scheme of renovations and redecorations in 1951 brought the

Webster Memorial Hall more into keeping with the needs of a Royal burgh. A young comic called JIMMY TARBUCK and the harmony trio of BACHELORS were headliners before the evergreen ALEXANDER BROTHERS made their professional debut at Arbroath in 1958. Reconstructed and enlarged in 1970, the town's theatre and cultural centre provides seating for 450 in the hall and 184 in the balcony. Angus and Down Productions gave us "Holiday Hayrides" with comedian FRANK CARSON telling 'em his way, singer DAVID KINNAIRD, and dancer BENNY GARCIA from the "Black & White Minstrel Show". More recently concerts led by singer ANNE LORNE GILLIES have caught the Arbroath public's imagination.

Two of Scotland's best known sons of show business, HARRY LAUDER and ANDY STEWART, spent their informative years in Arbroath and knew the High Street hall before attaining world-wide acclaim as ambassadors of traditional Scottish light entertainment.

Chapter Fourteen

"Highland Fling"

Inverness

Inverness

Early records tell us that plays and music hall turns were presented at a theatre situated near the junction of Inglis Street and Hamilton Street (formerly named Theatre Lane) prior to the establishment of the Theatre Royal in Bank Street in 1886. The New Theatre Royal, as it was always termed, favoured more cultural productions, but it was when Scotland's greatest character comedian WILL FYFFE was in revue that the theatre was destroyed by fire on 17th March, 1931. His considerable wardrobe of costumes and props were lost in the devastation, but in the best thespian tradition the show went on the following day in the Central Hall Picture House, precursor of the Empire Theatre.

Erected in Academy Street in 1912 for the exhibition of films, this building was converted into the Empire Theatre on 17th September, 1934, when an enlarged stage and dressing rooms were provided. Thus, the owners Caledonian Associated Cinemas Ltd., had made good the loss of the Theatre Royal within four years. For the next 36 years it housed opera, revue, variety, pantomime, plays, amateur drama festivals, dancing displays and wrestling contests.

The list of Scottish entertainers at the Empire is formidable — HARRY LAUDER; CHARLIE KEMBLE; TOMMY LORNE; GEORGE WEST; PETE MARTIN; JIMMY LOGAN; ALEC FINLAY; JOHNNY BEATTIE; ROBERT WILSON; CHIC MURRAY & MAIDIE; DUN-CAN MACRAE; RENEE HOUSTON & DONALD STEWART; the CORRIES and JOE GORDON FOLK FOUR. Appropriately for a Highland venue it was two Mod gold medallists, ALASDAIR GILLIES and CALUM KENNEDY who made the greatest impact. They each appeared at the Empire more often than any other personalities, and the record for the highest number of seats occupied belongs to the popular son of Stornoway CALUM KENNEDY.

The Empire's gala final night was attended by over 1000 on Saturday, 28th November, 1970. Compered by Ron Coburn whose career has encompassed every facet of the business from call boy, comics' foil and promoter of "Breath of Scotland" ceilidhs at home and abroad, the local groups of amateurs were not eclipsed by the professionals — baritone BILL McCUE, accordionist WILL STARR; and Muir of Ord comedian JOHNNY BOGAN. The orchestra was led by JOHN WORTH, manager of the Empire for its last 20 years.

Live theatre returned to the Highland capital when the controversial Eden Court complex opened in 1976, but variety enthusiasts have had to make do with infrequent one night stands in a venue where the output is predominantly films and plays.

Index of Artistes

A

B

C